VOLUME THREE

Comfort From

Meditations

For Such a Time as This

EPISTLES

NORTHWESTERN PUBLISHING HOUSE
Milwaukee, Wisconsin

Scripture taken from the

HOLY BIBLE, NEW INTERNATIONAL VERSION

Copyright © 1973, 1978, 1984 International Bible Society

Used by permission of Zondervan Bible Publishers.

Library of Congress Card 90-64-163
Northwestern Publishing House
1250 N. 113th St., Milwaukee, WI 53226-3284
© 1991 by Northwestern Publishing House
Published 1991
Printed in the United States of America

CONTENTS

Through Suffering to Glory

The Wonderful Ways of God

A Matter of Death and Life

Children in God's Family

A Call to Prayer

The Disciple Looks to the Future

Divine Counsel for Troubled Christians

God's Grace in Our Lives

Living in Hope

Living in Confidence

EDITOR'S PREFACE

For Such a Time as This. The title of this three volume set of devotions comes from a thought that Mordecai brought to Queen Esther's attention during days of trial and tribulation for the Old Testament people of God. "For such a time as this," Mordecai suggested, God had placed Esther in a position of honor and influence so she could bring God's promised help to God's people (Esther 4:14).

For Such a Time as This. Days of trial and tribulation are no strangers to God's people today. Trials and troubles challenge us, spiritual enemies beset us, fiery trials scorch our faith, our own frailty and mortality frightens us, tragic losses mount, guilt plagues our consciences, personal problems put us on the verge of despair, and sometimes even daily life seems difficult and discouraging.

For Such a Time as This. In times such as these Christians of all ages have turned to God in prayer seeking his help, his promised deliverance, his comfort. They have turned to his Word to find what he has to say to them, and for the past thirty-three years *Meditations* has helped to lead Christians to that comfort of God's Word. Comfort in the fact that God knows who we are, where we are, what we are. Comfort in that God knows the story of our lives and has seen to it through Jesus Christ that it has a happy ending. Comfort in that Jesus has promised to guide us through every trouble, even through the valley of the shadow of death, until we safely stand with him at God's right hand.

For Such a Time as This. Now 300 of those messages of comfort have been selected for inclusion in these three volumes. Each volume contains 100 devotions based on texts chosen from the Gospels, the Epistles, and the Old Testament. Pastor Henry Paustian of Watertown, Wisconsin read through some 12,045 devotions and selected the best of these comfort meditations. Minor changes have been made in some of the original devotions to bring them into line with current procedures. All Scripture quotations and citations are from the NIV; capitalization and punctuation principles reflect current style; titles now are solely the themes of individual devotions instead of a weekly series.

For Such a time as This. Note that on the cover the letters "h-i-s" in the word **this** are printed in another color. That was done to remind all of us that no matter in what situation we may find ourselves, this is still **his,** God's time, that our lives and the events in our lives happen not by chance but under the providential direction of our Father in heaven. As the cover illustration further indicates, we are always safe in his hands.

May the reader find God's comfort in these devotions.

Lyle Albrecht

In this you greatly rejoice, though now for a little while you may have had to suffer grief in all kinds of trials. These have come so that your faith—of greater worth than gold, which perishes even though refined by fire—may be proved genuine and may result in praise, glory and honor when Jesus Christ is revealed. (1 Peter 1:6,7)

THANK GOD YOU'RE TESTED

A test involves pressure. Whether an engine, a structural beam or a person is being tested, the method is the same. Pressure or stress of some kind is applied to the object of the test. Without stress, the test wouldn't really be a test. Giving a second-grade math test to high school seniors wouldn't be a true test.

The purpose of all testing is the same, too. A test is meant to discover any weakness so that it can be corrected, so that the product (whatever it is) can be improved. If the object passes the test, of course, it has been proven to be genuine, the real thing. It is fit for its purpose.

Now we see why the Apostle Peter speaks so highly of trials in the Christian's life. They are all important tests of our faith, and they have wonderful results, because God's own purpose is behind them.

Even while we rejoice in our eternal inheritance, Peter says, we may be suffering grief in all kinds of trials. Sometimes the cross—suffering because of our confession of Christ. Sometimes the loss—of people or things dear to us. Sometimes physical pain and weakness, or disappointment or another kind of trouble.

Difficult, yes! Distressing, yes! But thank God when you're tested! For it is your gracious God himself who tests your faith. He himself is in the test. He applies pressure to reveal and to correct any weakness. And if he brings you through the fire of affliction, it is not to harm you, but only to refine, to purify, to temper and to strengthen your faith.

"One Christian who has been tried," wrote Luther, "is worth a hundred who have not been tried, for the blessing of God grows in trials. . . . When faith is thus tried, all that is dross and false must pass off and drop away. Then will result a glorious reward, praise and commendation when Christ will be revealed."

It's great to be alive, even when you're being tested in the fire, for your loving God is purifying and proving your faith. He is refining and strengthening it for your eternal benefit. You can indeed thank God when you're tested and continue to "rejoice."

Lord Jesus, help me to rejoice even in my trials, and to come through every test with a stronger and better faith. Amen.

I consider that our present sufferings are not worth comparing with the glory that will be revealed in us. (Romans 8:18)

A WORD ABOUT SUFFERING

Suffering is a fact of life. It strikes young and old, rich and poor. Its root cause is sin. We all suffer from sicknesses and diseases because we live in a sinful world. Who could describe all the forms of physical, mental and spiritual suffering as they exist in our world today?

Thank God that in his suffering Servant he has given us an answer to suffering. Our Substitute suffered it all. He suffered trial, temptation, poverty, pain, sorrow, rejection and death. He was indeed a man who was familiar with suffering. Jesus suffered so that we would not have to suffer the eternal torments of hell.

That accomplished fact directly affects our view, as God's people, on suffering. By faith in Christ we know that God is our loving Father. In our Father's hand suffering is a tool by which he would draw us closer to himself, train us or give us an opportunity to witness to his undeserved love.

Many of us have experienced passing through a period of suffering. We learned from that experience that man's life truly does not consist in the amount of things he possesses. God's promises became even more valuable, and in that way he drew us closer to himself

We all experience the suffering which our Father sends into our lives as discipline. Scripture says, "God disciplines us for our good, that we may share in his holiness. No discipline seems pleasant at the time, but painful. Later on, however, it produces a harvest of righteousness and peace for those who have been trained by it."

Sometimes God permits suffering to come upon us so that by faithful patience and endurance we might witness to others. Seldom do we think of suffering as an opportunity, but often that's what it is.

In the middle of suffering we can at times lose perspective. Our word about life for today puts all suffering into perspective. When all is said and done, it isn't worth comparing with the heavenly glory and joy that awaits us. We have God's Word for that.

Should Thy mercy send me
Sorrow, toil and woe,
Or should pain attend me
On my path below,
Grant that I may never
Fail Thy hand to see;
Grant that I may ever
Cast my care on Thee. Amen.

To keep me from becoming conceited because of these surpassingly great revelations, there was given me a thorn in my flesh, a messenger of Satan, to torment me. (2 Corinthians 12:7)

A THORN IN THE FLESH

It's very difficult to look upon troubles and afflictions, sufferings and hardships—those unpleasant aspects of our lives—as being connected at all with God's grace. "Why is God doing this to me?" is the first question that comes to mind. "What am I being punished for? What wrong have I done?"

In the throes of suffering we are tempted to question the grace and mercy of God, even his fairness and justice. "How can this come from the hand of a loving Lord?"

Job searched for an answer to his sufferings. He could only come up with the same questions, until God revealed the truth.

That the Lord never withdraws his loving hand from his children and that we are always the objects of his gracious care are assurances of which we need to be reminded constantly. We draw such assurance from God's Word. "For the Lord will not reject his people; he will never forsake his inheritance." It is his promise, "Never will I leave you; never will I forsake you."

The Apostle Paul was given a thorn in his flesh—a particular kind of affliction. We don't know the exact nature of it, but it was something that troubled him considerably. He said it kept him from being conceited because of the great revelations he had received. He also described it as a messenger of Satan to torment him.

Can a messenger of Satan given to torment someone be consistent with God's loving care? Can it be a manifestation of his grace? Paul saw it as that, not because it was a reasonable way to look at it, but because his faith had grown to trust his Lord's concern for him in everything that happened to him. He knew God had a purpose, a good purpose for allowing him to suffer this affliction.

In that faith Paul could assert so positively, "We know that in all things God works for the good of those who love him, who have been called according to his purpose."

God deals with his children today no differently than he did with Paul. He has not made us immune to sufferings, to afflictions or trials, but we can be certain that those difficult times in our lives are not for our harm but come with the Lord's knowledge and will serve the good purpose he has in mind for us.

Gracious Lord, we trust your love in the good things you give us. Help us to see your love in adversity, too. Amen.

3

I consider that our present sufferings are not worth comparing with the glory that will be revealed in us. (Romans 8:18)

NO COMPARISON

Cancer! Heart-attack! Bankruptcy! What do these three seemingly unrelated items have in common? They all identify sufferings of one kind or another. We see these sufferings all around us. Friends, relatives and even we ourselves may have experienced them in our lives.

The Apostle Paul was well acquainted with sufferings. He tells us, "Five times I received from the Jews forty lashes minus one. Three times I was beaten with rods, once I was stoned, three times I was shipwrecked, I spent a night and a day in the open sea." Yet in spite of all these problems, Paul was not discouraged or fed up with life. He looked beyond his present situation to the glories which would be his in heaven. For Paul there was no comparison between his present suffering and his future glory. All the pain, grief and heartaches of this life were quickly replaced as Paul thought of sharing in Christ's glory in heaven.

Is our life much different from Paul's? We may suffer under different circumstances than Paul did. Nevertheless, suffering and grief in varying degrees have affected all of us. We cannot escape it in this life. The cause of all suffering, sin, is as much a part of our world today as it was of Paul's world. Ever since the fall of man into sin, suffering has been an ever present part of man's life. At times though it receives too much attention. We rob ourselves of the joy which is ours by faith in Christ.

While sin has brought suffering into this world, Christ has made us heirs of a glorious inheritance in heaven. Through faith we have become the children of God. Just preceding our verse St. Paul reminds us that "we are heirs—heirs of God and coheirs with Christ, if indeed we share in his sufferings in order that we may also share in his glory." To share in Christ's glory is beyond description. Everything that we consider beautiful and glorious today, is still infected with sin. How much more beautiful and glorious eternity is, we shall simply have to wait and see.

St. John described some of the beauty of that eternal glory when he wrote, "Never again will they hunger; never again will they thirst. The sun will not beat upon them, nor any scorching heat. . . . And God will wipe away every tear from their eyes." There's no comparison! As we endure the sufferings of this life, let us look forward to future glory in Christ.

O Lord, be with me in all the sufferings of this life that I may share in eternal glories with you. Amen.

In this you greatly rejoice, though now for a little while you may have had to suffer grief in all kinds of trials. These have come so that your faith . . . may be proved genuine and result in praise, glory and honor when Jesus Christ is revealed. (1 Peter 1:6,7)

STRENGTH IN TRIALS

When things are not going quite right, a bit of advice frequently handed out is to keep a stiff upper lip. The advice suggests that there are certain difficulties you can expect in life, and the only way to cope with them is to grit your teeth and make the best of it.

The Christian has a different view of life's difficulties. First of all, he understands their origin. They result from sin. All problems, all suffering, all sorrows, all difficulties, all misery, all frustrations have a common origin. They result from sin. Sin has contaminated the whole human race, and the believer also suffers from that contamination.

In addition, the Christian has another view of the difficulties he encounters in life. He knows that they are under God's control and that they are intended for his good. Granted, there are times when this is extremely hard to understand and accept. Yet the Bible stresses this again and again. God sends corrective measures into our lives, just as parents do with their children. Peter wrote to his readers that the trials which they were encountering had come "so that your faith . . . may be proved genuine and result in praise, glory and honor when Jesus Christ is revealed."

God's love for us is so great that he wants nothing to lure us from living and abiding in his saving grace. It is our trials in life, our problems, our tribulations which keep us from becoming too wrapped up in worldly affairs. If everything went along smoothly in life, if every day brought nothing but joy and pleasure, if every week and every month were nothing but one big pleasure trip, we would face the grave danger of becoming very attached to this world.

But we are strangers on this earth. Heaven is our home. The trials of life remind us of this. With the strength God provides, we can endure these trials. The resurrection of Jesus Christ from the dead is God's assurance that he will give us that strength. This is a very important part of our living Easter hope. How rich we are that God strengthens us in all the trials of life!

O Lord, grant us strength as we encounter the trials and difficulties of life. Help us realize that they serve our good and will continue only for a short season until we live with you in heaven. Amen.

For you were like sheep going astray, but now you have returned to the Shepherd and Overseer of your souls. (1 Peter 2:25)

WANDERERS AT HOME

The picture Peter portrays for us here is not as vivid for us as it must have been for his first readers. Most of us do not live in a farming community as many of our grandparents did. And even fewer of us have ever raised sheep.

Sheep have a terrible tendency to wander. It's not that they're so curious to find out what the rest of the world looks like. It's just that they tend to become so preoccupied with what they're doing that they don't pay any attention to where they are. If a sheep is grazing, he simply keeps his head down and goes from one good clump of grass to another. If he's not carefully watched, he will just keep walking and eating until he becomes hopelessly lost. Alone and helpless he is then choice prey for any wild animal.

That's exactly the way it is also for those who are not under the watchful eye and protecting staff of the Good Shepherd, Jesus. They simply wander around, go from one earthly pleasure to another and are unaware of any danger. They too are choice prey for the devil, who "prowls around like a roaring lion looking for someone to devour" (1 Peter 5:8).

We too were once in that situation, lost and helpless and in danger. But we are no longer. Through the life and death of Jesus Christ we have been brought back into the shelter of his protecting arms. Once again we have a Shepherd and Overseer for our souls. Gently he leads us toward our eternal home, always aware of our helpless condition.

In times of suffering how comforting it is to know that we're not alone. Jesus is still there to care for us and to guide everything so that it serves our welfare. Every day he leads us back from wandering and another step closer to our eternal home in heaven. With a shepherd such as this we are of all people truly blessed—even in sufferings.

Jesus, the Good Shepherd, lead me in the paths of righteousness and keep me in your protecting arms. Comfort me with your word and finally deliver me from all evil by taking me to be with you in heaven. Amen.

The creation waits in eager expectation for the sons of God to be revealed. But if we hope for what we do not yet have, we wait for it patiently. (Romans 8:19,25)

PATIENCE ON THE ROAD TO GLORY

In an age of "instant gratification" people find it hard to wait. But "wait patiently" is what Christians are told to do when they are burdened by trials and sufferings of all kinds.

God's whole creation has been crippled by the effects of sin. And Christians are not immune to these troubles. Even though we have become children of God through faith in Jesus, the redemption of our bodies is still unfulfilled. That means they continue to fall into sin. And they still experience disease and handicaps of all kinds. Sin and its consequences are evident in the life of every Christian.

But the promise of God is that a day is coming when also the physical world will be set free from the effects of sin. All creation "will be liberated from its bondage to decay and brought into the glorious freedom of the children of God." Our own bodies cry out for that day of redemption. So for now we must wait for these things. We wait in the knowledge that God will most certainly keep the promises he has made.

Being patient in time of trouble will not take away the trouble. But as we wait in faith and hope, our attitude toward our trouble can change. We see the trouble as part of God's righteous judgment on a world of sin. We see it as temporary. We see it as something that will end when God completes the work of redemption that has already freed us from the guilt of our sins.

How patient are we while we wait? Patience is certainly not easy. Days and years of suffering go by very slowly. Sometimes the loss is so overwhelming we can hardly think about anything else. Who can be patient in such circumstances?

God's Word encourages us by comparing present sufferings with future glory. The more we concentrate on the glory, the more we will be able to endure the sufferings.

Be patient and await his leisure
In cheerful hope, with heart content
To take whate'er thy Father's pleasure
And his discerning love hath sent.

Dear Father, grant me patience while I wait for the glorious day when all my troubles will come to an end. Amen.

And the God of all grace, who called you to his eternal glory in Christ, after you have suffered a little while, will himself restore you and make you strong, firm and steadfast. (1 Peter 5:10)

THE WHOLESOME EFFECT OF SUFFERING

There is no end to what the ungodly will suffer in hell. And what they suffer here on earth is but a preview of their damnation. To us, who look to Christ for our salvation, however, the misery of this life is a preview of what we shall escape. For us it is a wholesome sorrow, by which God refines our faith and preserves our hope.

No matter what may befall us here, our God is still "the God of all grace, who called you to his eternal glory in Christ." He is still with us. He still feeds, shelters and protects us. He still forgives our sins and assures us of our eternal inheritance.

Knowing that we have a Father in heaven, what do we have to fear on earth? Since God is for us, who can oppose us? Even if the thorns of Satan tear at our flesh and inflict the worst physical pain and mental anguish, we know that they cannot touch our soul. Nothing can sever us from the love and promises of Christ.

Even if it were our lot to writhe on a bed of pain for a thousand years, we still would be able to shout victoriously with Paul, "Who shall separate us from the love of Christ? Shall trouble or hardship or persecution or famine or nakedness or danger or sword? As it is written: 'For your sake we face death all day long; we are considered as sheep to be slaughtered. No, in all these things we are more than conquerors through him who loved us. For I am convinced that neither death nor life, neither angels nor demons, neither the present nor the future, nor any powers, neither height nor depth, nor anything else in all creation, will be able to separate us from the love of God that is in Christ Jesus our Lord.' " (Romans 8:35-39).

God is merciful and kind. He will not let us suffer beyond our ability. But he does let suffering come when it is for our good. Like a loving, faithful father,he chastises us in order to rid us of our foolishness and to save us from disaster. In a marvelous way, he uses those same sorrows (which give the ungodly a foretaste of hell) in order to perfect, establish, strengthen and settle us on our way to eternal glory.

Dear Lord Jesus, do not let us despair when suffering comes, but cause it to perfect our faith and to strengthen our hope in you. Amen.

Don't be deceived, my dear brothers. Every good and perfect gift is from above, coming down from the Father of the heavenly lights, who does not change like shifting shadows. (James 1:16,17)

LOOK TO THE SOURCE OF YOUR BLESSINGS!

James wrote his letter to the church at a time when persecution was her close companion. So his words are immediately fresh and powerful and apply to every Christian of every time in every place. For when has Satan ever gone to sleep or ceased to voice his hatred for the Body of Christ and its members? Or when has the world, which is in bondage to Satan, ever stopped opposing the church and the gospel? Our enemies may change their tactics from generation to generation, but not their purpose.

As a man who knew the meaning of persecution and temptation, James was equipped to rally our courage and to cheer us. "Consider it pure joy," he said, "whenever you face trials of many kinds, because you know that the testing of your faith develops perseverance. Perseverance must finish its work so that you may be mature and complete, not lacking anything"; and "blessed is the man who perseveres under trial, because when he has stood the test, he will receive the victor's crown of life that God has promised to those who love him" (James 1:2-4,12).

So in his opening chapter James not only lifts our thoughts up and away from our present suffering, but he also bids them to dwell on the crown of glory awaiting us in heaven and on the one who has prepared it for us. In one short statement he recalls both the love and the great power of the God we worship. He is the "Father of lights"—the source of every good and perfect gift. He is our Creator, who separated the light from the darkness and has promised that, as surely as the sun will rise on schedule, he will continue to provide for our earthly needs. He is our Redeemer, Jesus Christ, who came as the very Light of the World to free us from death, hell and the "prince of darkness." He is the Holy Spirit, who has illuminated our hearts with the light of the gospel and has given us the sure hope of eternal life.

So let the trials come! Let the devil roar. Let him open his jaws and gape at us. Let the whole world disapprove of us and vent their displeasure. These are things which James and all of the apostles teach us we can expect here as members of the Body of Christ. But these are things which even add to our joy; for they are evidence that we are not the children of this world, but the children of a heavenly Father and the heirs of every good and perfect gift.

Dear Father in heaven, continue to bless us, for Jesus' sake. Amen.

Now if we are children, then we are heirs—heirs of God and co-heirs with Christ, if indeed we share in his sufferings in order that we may also share in his glory. (Romans 8:17)

THROUGH SUFFERING TO GLORY

With one bold stroke of his pen, the inspired Apostle Paul summarizes our new relationship with God in Christ. Eloquently he leads us through an understanding of our present status and carries us to the very gates of heaven.

The Holy Spirit has graciously called us to believe the Gospel of Christ. Through that saving Word he enlightens us, purifies us and preserves our faith in him. Therefore, according to that same Word, we are rightly called the "children" of God. But who can fathom all that this implies! Even the wise and aged John had to pause in amazement at the thought and declared "How great is the love the Father has lavished on us, that we should be called children of God (1 John 3:1).

"And if we are children, then we are heirs," Paul continues, "heirs of God and co-heirs with Christ." We, who were at one time no people at all, now have the unspeakable honor of being called the people of God. By our sins we deserved to inherit the whirlwind of his wrath. But now we possess the promise of an inheritance which makes the wealthiest man on earth look like a wretched beggar by comparison. For Jesus' sake, we have become heirs of eternal life. All who believe in him will never die.

"If indeed we share in his sufferings in order that we may also share in his glory," Paul concludes. It is impossible to escape suffering in this hostile world. Christ suffered here, and so will we. "A student is not above his teacher, nor a servant above his master" (Matthew 10:24). Paul makes it clear: no suffering, no glory.

But "our present sufferings are not worth comparing with the glory that will be revealed in us" (Romans 8:18). Who of us can imagine the glories of heaven! "However, as it is written: 'No eye has seen, no ear has heard, no mind has conceived what God has prepared for those who love him' " (1 Corinthians 2:9). With our eyes of flesh we look around us and see nothing but temptations, disease, death and decay. With our ears of flesh we hear about wars, earthquakes, fires and floods. But with our eyes and ears of faith we hear of God's mercy and forgiveness in Christ and look forward to the glory which shall be revealed in us.

O Holy Spirit, give us the strength to bear whatever suffering comes our way, and refresh us through the blessed hope of eternal life; for Jesus' sake. Amen.

How unsearchable his judgments, and his paths beyond tracing out!
(Romans 11:33)

WHEN MY FOOLISH HEART ASKS WHY

How many people don't approach life in the same way that Beethoven departed it—shaking his fist at the sky! They complain that life isn't fair. They look for someone to blame and inevitably point at God. They consider the constant threat or presence of war, famine, natural disaster and human injustice; and they conclude that either there is no God or that he is a harsh and unreasonable tyrant. Even we, who are Christians, are often tempted to complain and to ask why: "Why must I, a faithful member of the church, suffer with cancer?" "Why did my husband have to die, while so many immoral men go on living?" "Why was our child born with a handicap?"

The world cannot produce a satisfactory answer. And where the Bible gives us an answer, the children of men refuse to accept it. We all know the temptation to doubt that God's purposes are good, for we are all made of the same flesh. And our natural mind of flesh is opposed to God and his word. Besides this, Satan is continually at our backs and whispering, "Yea, hath God said? Does God really mean it when he says that he loves you? Why, look at all you are suffering! Do you really think God means to bring something good out of this?"

When thoughts like this come to us, let us recognize them as the lies of Satan. God has already given us all the answers we need in his holy Word. So we can turn and say: "Satan, get out of here! My God has never promised me a perfect life of bliss on this earth. And when suffering comes my way, it is only further evidence of his truth and love. He is teaching me not to fall in love with this world and drawing me closer to himself and to his promises in Christ. And even if I am about to die, you cannot touch me. For my Redeemer lives, and he will raise me from the dead again and give me eternal life.

"I cannot say exactly why or how all the events of my life fit into God's overall plan. But that is none of my business. For 'My thoughts are not your thoughts, neither are your ways my ways, declares the Lord' (Isaiah 55:8). 'Our God is in heaven; he does whatever pleases him' (Psalm 115:3). And that is good enough for me. For I know that he was pleased to send me a Savior from sin. And 'He who did not spare his own Son, but gave him up for us all—how will he not also, along with him, graciously give us all things?' " (Romans 8:32)

When my foolish heart asks why, quiet me with your words, "Be still, and know that I am God." Amen.

11

Who has been his counselor? (Romans 11:34)

SOME GOOD ADVICE

Downcast and dejected, the man stepped into the counselor's office. "What seems to be the trouble?" the counselor asked. "I don't know exactly. All I know is that I'm not happy. Is there anything you can suggest to help me?" The counselor looked at the man for a moment and then he said, "I hear a famous comedian is in town playing to a packed house every evening. They say people come away from his performance holding their sides from laughing so hard. Why don't you go to his performance tonight and forget your troubles?" The man looked down at the floor for a moment, and then he said, "Sir, I am that comedian."

That counselor's advice was as wrong and foolish as the kind of advice people sometimes like to give God. Some would like to advise God that he doesn't really understand human nature and the times in which we live when he forbids marital unfaithfulness, perversion and fornication. They suggest that God's words are impractical and out of date. They would like to tell God that sin isn't as serious as he has said it is, and that the punishment for sin surely shouldn't be something as severe as eternal punishment in hell. God ought to relax his standards today, they insist.

Then, too, they would like to advise God that he has made the way to heaven too restrictive. Anyone who is sincere and honest and tries to do what is right ought to be able to go to heaven, they feel. "Can't we be considered Christians without believing everything the Bible says?" they ask. "How important is belief in the Bible's account of creation or the virgin birth or the resurrection from the dead?" As ridiculous as it sounds, they suppose that they can counsel almighty God!

But that's turning things completely around. It is God who is our Counselor. On the night of his betrayal Jesus promised to send his disciples another Counselor who would be with them forever. That Counselor is the Holy Spirit, who advises and counsels us by means of the Scriptures. He informs us that our sins are many, that they are serious, and that they indeed deserve eternal punishment. But he also assures us that God has declared us righteous for the sake of the innocent sufferings and death of the Savior. He comforts us with the knowledge that God will make everything in life serve a good purpose for us and that he will take us to heaven. That is good counsel—the kind of counsel that the comedian needed too!

Lord, help me always to listen attentively to the counsel of your holy Word. Amen.

Oh, the depth of the riches of the wisdom and knowledge of God! (Romans 11:33)

THE FATHER KNOWS BEST

"**M**y daddy knows everything!" At least that's what I thought at age five. He could fix anything, make everything right. He had answers for all my questions. I don't think Dad grew stupid while I got smart; but at fifteen I was no longer sure that father knew best. At twenty-five, though, I was ready to go back to him for advice.

Likewise the Christian with a childlike faith knows that his heavenly Father knows best. It is the spiritual adolescent who questions God's wisdom and knowledge. But Christians, matured by Scripture and experience, recover that childlike awe, and with St. Paul they marvel, "Oh, the depth of the riches of the wisdom and knowledge of God!"

How far God's wisdom and knowledge are above our own! The current arguments and ideas of men may sound good. They claim to offer quick and easy answers to life's problems, immediate gratification for human desires, simplified explanations for the events and purposes of life. So we look around us in this world. We see something that we like and immediately think that it must be good for us—simply because we like it. God, on the other hand, is able to see far beyond our likes and dislikes. And, like a good father, he permits his children to receive only that which is best for them in the end, whether for the moment they like it or not. Patience discovers the wisdom of God and exposes the folly of men.

Only on the Sixth Day could the perfect wisdom of God be seen in his Creation. Only on Easter could the perfect wisdom of God be seen in his plan of salvation. Only in eternity will we fully see what the wisdom of God has accomplished in the life and world through which he now leads us. Until then we will find comfort and joy only in trusting the answers he has already worked out for our good; and by praising him for his vast and hidden wisdom.

Yes, God knows everything. That means he also knows us. God knows our sins and weaknesses. Long before we were born, he foresaw our predicament and determined in love to send us a Savior from sin. And that Savior is Jesus Christ, the good Shepherd, who laid down his life for the sheep, and who said of us before we were born, "My sheep listen to my voice; I know them, and they follow me. I give them eternal life" (John 10:27,28).

Dear Lord and Savior, teach us to trust in you alone and to depend on your wisdom and judgment. Amen.

Humble yourselves, therefore, under God's mighty hand, that he may lift you up in due time. (1 Peter 5:6)

GOD'S TIME IS THE BEST TIME

We all have days, even weeks and months, when everything in life seems to be going our way. But then suddenly, altogether unexpectedly, everything shifts into reverse. One day the sun is shining brightly; the next day all is dark and overcast. One week we are actively carrying out our responsibilities; the next week we are lying helpless on a hospital bed. Every day the world turns over on someone who has just been sitting on top of it.

Where is there a Christian who has not had this kind of an experience? Where is there a Christian who has never asked: "If God can let suffering and sorrow come that quickly into my life, why won't he remove it just as quickly?"

Often people deeply resent it when suffering or sorrow disrupt their blissful plans. They grow bitter and cynical and consider the temptation to curse God and die. But God has given us a powerful weapon against these temptations in the Scriptures. In our devotional text the Apostle Peter gives a special word of encouragement.

God is the Lord. He rules his creation with a "mighty hand." So doesn't he know what he is doing when he lets suffering come? And doesn't he also know when it is best to remove it? "Humble yourselves, therefore, under God's mighty hand," Peter writes, "that he may lift you up in due time."

When we pray to God in our time of need, we may do so with confidence, knowing that the God who sent his Son to die for us certainly will also hear and answer our prayers. Sometimes the answer may be yes; sometimes it may be no. Most often, experience has taught us, the answer is "Wait!"

God's ways certainly are not our ways. Nor is his time our time. And how long his "due time" usually seems to linger! But our comfort lies in the fact that it is his time—a time not established by our nearsighted emotions, but by his far-reaching wisdom.

Someone once said there are two ways to open a flower bud. You can force the petals apart (and, in doing so, destroy the flower), or you can leave it alone until God slowly, but surely, unfolds it. By ranting and complaining we can hinder our own blessings. But by patiently depending on Christ and his mercy, we will never be disappointed. "Humble yourselves, therefore, under God's mighty hand, that he may lift you up in due time."

Help us, O Lord, patiently to bear all things; for Jesus sake. Amen.

They passed the first and second guards and came to the iron gate leading to the city. It opened for them by itself, and they went through it. When they had walked the length of one street, suddenly the angel left him. Then Peter came to himself and said, "Now I know without a doubt that the Lord sent his angel and rescued me from Herod's clutches and from everything the Jewish people were anticipating." (Acts 12:10,11)

GOD'S MASTER PLAN

When we look ahead, life is a blur. Even as we experience it, life is usually out of focus. But when we look back, we often see life with 20-20 vision.

This is what Peter discovered when the angel left him. Sitting in prison, Peter had placed his life in the Lord's hands without really knowing what would happen. Even while he was participating in the escape, he was only dimly conscious of what was going on. But once outside the prison, after the angel had left him, he could see one thing clearly in all that happened: the Lord's hand.

Peter's observation also holds true for the rest of the early church. When Jesus ascended to heaven, the disciples knew that Jesus had commissioned them to bring the gospel to all lands. But they had no idea how it would happen. Now Peter could look back and see a pattern in all that happened. Pentecost, the preaching of the gospel to the Gentiles, even persecution itself—all was directed by the Lord as part of his master plan.

Christians may look back on all of history and clearly see the guiding hand of the Lord. In his first recorded sermon, the Apostle Paul emphasized that God directed the affairs of Israel to make possible the coming of the Savior. We also observe that it was no accident that the mighty Caesar Augustus issued the taxation decree. As a result, prophecy was fulfilled, and the Savior was born in Bethlehem. It was no accident that the persecutions sent the Christians from the city of Jerusalem. As a result they carried the saving gospel with them to people far away.

All Christians can look back on life and see the Lord's guiding hand. God has arranged lives to bring Christians to faith and to strengthen them in it. The chance acquaintance and the passing event may have seemed of no importance at the time. Years later the Christian sees how the Lord arranged them for the believer's eternal welfare. Only heaven itself will reveal how carefully the Lord has guided us along the way.

Help me in life and death, O God,
Help me through Jesus' dying blood;
Help me as thou hast helped me. Amen.

For the eyes of the Lord are on the righteous and his ears are attentive to their prayer, but the face of the Lord is against those who do evil. (1 Peter 3:1,2)

HE WATCHES OVER US

The heathen do not expend any effort to bring up their children in God's ways. They have no reservations about flying in the face of God's Commandments. And they not only "get by" with it but even earn the respect of many people. There almost appears to be a rule that the wicked will prosper and the righteous suffer.

Are not these thoughts similar to what must have gone through Job's mind? Within a short time, everything went wrong for him. He lost his holdings to bands of thieves. His children died in a storm. His wife blamed and rejected him. False friends increased his misery by suggesting that God was punishing him for some evil deed.

Why do the righteous suffer? God tells us that it is according to his will, and that he will not abandon us in our suffering. He did not merely plan some distant salvation for us and then leave us to grope our way through life alone. He has also promised to protect and to care for us in spite of our suffering, even while we are in the midst of it. And that is good enough for us!

We cannot see God. He is a spirit. His being and his ways are beyond our comprehension. When Job began to wonder why God lets the righteous suffer, God taught him a valuable lesson. He said, "Can you really understand my ways, Job? Where were you when I laid the foundation of the world ? Where were you when I made the ox and measured out the first crocodile?" and Job answered, "I know that you can do all things" (Job 42:2). Job conceded to the will and wisdom of God.

The Lord, our God, can do all things. In loving kindness he keeps watch over us night and day. He hears and sees everything that our enemies try to do against us. If anyone harms us, his ear is quick to catch our faintest sigh. "For the eyes of the Lord are over the righteous, and his ears are open to their prayers."

Should we then be concerned when we see that the wicked prosper here on earth? Let God himself give the answer on the day of judgment. In the long run, evil will receive its reward. Our God is still in heaven, and his "face . . . is against those who do evil." But we can live in cheerful confidence. For we have learned to know him as our gracious God and Redeemer, who watches over us and answers our prayers. Let us follow him.

Lord God, remind us of your watchful presence and refresh us on our way through this valley of tears till we reach our home at last. Amen.

Who has known the mind of the Lord? Or who has been his counselor? (Romans 11:34)

RELY ON GOD'S PERFECT WISDOM

"**G**od doesn't know what he's doing." When things do not happen the way we think they should, we are tempted to question God's ways. "Why, God?" We angrily demand that he explain himself and show us the justice of his actions. "Why do you permit so much evil and violence? How can you let so many babies be murdered before birth? Why did you let my parent become an alcoholic? Why did you let my sister get hooked on drugs? Why did you give me an unfaithful spouse? Why am I sick? God, you messed up again!"

Shall we blame God? Blame him for what? Incompetence, impotence or a lack of love and compassion? Perhaps God needs us to tell him how to run this universe. Our advice would soon straighten out this mess! If only we were in charge.

Oh, really? But what kind of counselors would we be? We are so selfish, so vengeful, so merciless and unforgiving.

For example, our Lord does not desire the "death of the wicked, but rather that they turn from their ways and live." Yet how often do we who have experienced this love still "damn" something or somebody? That curse slips out so easily, so thoughtlessly. What if God would take our advice when we damn our trick knee or when we damn our neighbor for whom Christ died, too?

Thank God he doesn't rely on our confused and self-centered counsel! How dare we challenge the all-knowing, all-wise and almighty Lord God? How dare we make him accountable to us?

We can trust the wisdom of the One who devised and executed salvation. He is our ever-faithful Savior-God, who assures us that nothing happens to us by chance. Our Lord also promises us that it is his unfailing love that controls all things in order to bless us. His perfect wisdom can even overrule sin and Satan, so that they must serve God's purposes. Even our cry, "Why, God?" will become a blessing for us if it drives us to his Word.

And if God chooses to veil the specific "why" of his actions, then let us humbly bow before his perfect wisdom, steadfastly relying on his eternal love. For how can we doubt our merciful Savior who gave his life to redeem us?

Precious Lord, who can understand why you would die to save us wretched sinners? Strengthen our faith greatly, so we trust your wisdom, not only for salvation but for all things. Amen.

Not many of you were wise by human standards; not many were influential; not many were of noble birth. (1 Corinthians 1:26)

WHO'S WHO—BEFORE GOD

"**W**hy, Lord, why?" That was the question the lady on the phone asked. She had just received news that her sister-in-law and two children had died. A train/car accident took their lives at an unmarked crossing.

The ever-recurring question is, "Why?" Just ask any parent. But other people ask it too. A Christian might ask, "Why me, Lord?" when considering the Lord's call to follow him in humble faith.

In the daily course of life, people are chosen for special favors because of who they are or what they have made of themselves or whom they know. One wouldn't expect to see the president of the United States standing at the end of a long line at the bank or supermarket. Authority, power and birth mean something before men.

Human reason might presume that God calls people to be members of his family of believers for the same reasons. But Paul reminded the Corinthian Christians that God's way of doing things is not comparable to man's. Few among them could lay claim to great wisdom, superior posi-

tions of authority or favored birth in noble families. Yet they were members of the family of believers.

Everything depends on God's grace. "It is by grace you have been saved, through faith—and this not from yourselves, it is the gift of God —not by works, so that no one can boast" (Ephesians 2:8,9).

God's undeserved love presented Jesus as Savior to a world lost in sin. God's undeserved love brought Jesus from the dead on that third day. God's undeserved love called us through his word to be members of his family through faith in Jesus Christ.

God's undeserved love moves him daily to keep us physically and spiritually as his children. And finally God's undeserved love for us will cause him to take our hand and walk with us through the doorway of death into the glory of our eternal home. Truly, by the grace of God alone, I am what I am—his child, an heir of his eternal heaven.

Forbid it, Lord, that I should boast
Save in the death of Christ, my God;
All the vain things that charm me most,
I sacrifice them to his blood.

Were the whole realm of nature mine
That were a tribute far too small;
Love so amazing, so divine,
Demands my soul, my life, my all. Amen.

And you also were included in Christ when you heard the word of truth, the gospel of your salvation. (Ephesians 1:13)

IF ONLY I HAD A STRONGER FAITH

"If only I had a faith like his!" People are often heard to make such a remark. But in admiring the faith of a fellow Christian, we dare not overlook the fact that we, too, have been greatly blessed by God. We, too, are a part of Christ's church. As Luther reminds us, "Jesus did not die only for Peter and Paul but also for you." And in the inspired words of St. Paul, "You also—as an individual—were included in Christ."

What an honor it is to be numbered along with great men and women of faith, people like Abraham, Paul, Peter, James, John and Mary! Yes, Christ's peace is also for you. You were "included in Christ."

Remember the Lord's life on earth. How often he left the crowds to heal or speak to one single person. On Calvary he not only prayed that the entire throng be forgiven their sinful, ignorant actions, but Jesus also assured an individual sinner, "Today you will be with me in paradise." After his resurrection Jesus appeared to the eleven disciples at once and to over 500 believers at one time. But he also met personally with Mary Magdalene.

At your baptism the triune God entered a covenant with you alone. Jesus was born, suffered, died and rose for you as an individual, just as much as for the entire race of mankind. God's peace was planned and performed for you. God's peace was performed to give you strength in every conflict with sin. God's peace is promised to you through "the word of truth, the gospel of your salvation." God's peace is given to you to comfort you in the midst of the many sorrows in life.

Yes, we may admire other Christians and look up to the Bible's heroes and heroines of faith. But let's not forget we have the same Savior and the same word of truth. May each of us grow in that word.

And may God's peace ever dwell in your heart and cause you to overflow with joy.

Chief of sinners though I be,
Jesus shed his blood for me;
Died that I might live on high,
Lived that I might never die.
As the branch is to the vine,
I am His, and He is mine. Amen.

We know that in all things God works for the good of those who love him, who have been called according to his purpose. (Romans 8:28)

GOD HAS A PLAN

At the beginning of the automobile assembly line an ugly piece of metal is forcefully attached to another piece of equally unattractive steel. A process begins. To a person who has never seen the finished product this scene might be viewed as a disastrous waste of time, material and machinery. But those who have seen the end of the assembly line know the final result, a brand new car. From this vantage point the beginning of the process makes sense.

More than 13,000 parts go into a car. Each has its specific place. If the auto worker attaches the wrong part, or forgets a part, or does a poor job of attaching it, the quality of the car is impaired. Maybe it won't run at all. Therefore each assembly-line worker must carefully follow his instructions to every minute detail.

In his eternal counsels God has prepared a blueprint for each one of us. "Called according to his purpose" means that our lives fit into his master plan. Right now the assembly line of our lives is in progress. The master planner is closely watching that assembly and is making sure that everything fits together perfectly piece by piece and step by step.

The assembly line of our lives does not end until we cross the threshold of heaven. The finished product is a life, totally perfected in every way, of eternal happiness. By faith we know what that finished product will be, even though our eyes have never seen it. As St. Paul says, "We live by faith, not by sight."

What a comfort to know that God has a plan for our lives and that we "have been called according to his purpose." With that understanding it is much easier to accept our troubles and bear with our tears. They are part of God's marvelous plan for us. We can't see the finished product now, but we know that it will be perfect and beautiful.

The remarkable thing is that God accomplishes his plan for us in spite of our sins. We often get in the way with our stubborn will and self-chosen deeds. It's only by grace that we are among those who love him and desire to have his plan fulfilled for our lives.

O Lord, help my faith to accept your plan for my life and not to stand in its way by my sins. I pray in my Redeemer's name. Amen.

And he died for all, that those who live should no longer live for themselves but for him who died for them and was raised again. (2 Corinthians 5:15)

A NEW VIEW OF DEATH

What is death? Most definitions view death as an end, the end of life, the end of biological functions, when it's all over and done.

Christ our Savior died and changed our view of death. He didn't change the scientific or physical nature of death, but the spiritual aspect of death has been radically changed. The original cause of death was removed when Christ died. And because he died for all, death has been conquered for all.

Dying started when sin entered the world, and since sin passes from one generation to the next, so does dying. Christ came and broke this deadly cycle. When he died, he took everyone's place and experienced once and for all that death which is sin's just punishment. He carried the sins of the world and paid for them by dying, not only physically, but by suffering all the wrath of a holy God against sin. That's what has changed everything and has given us a brand new life and a new view of death.

The old and natural view of death is that it is an awful and dreadful experience. Before Jesus conquered death for us, it hung over our heads as a menacing reality. Worst of all, it brought to mind the problem of finding ourselves face to face with God, whom we had offended in so many ways.

Now we have a new view of death. It still is frightening to us even though it has been conquered, but now we know that when we die, we aren't being punished. The death of Christ took care of that kind of death for us. Now we can see death as the way to a new life. Our death, thanks to the death and resurrection of Christ, is nothing more than a sleep from which we will awaken totally refreshed and glorified to live in the eternal mansions which Jesus went to prepare for us.

When Christ died, he rose again and so did we. We died with him as far as sin is concerned; when we were baptized, we were buried with him, and we also rose with him to a new life. Now we don't live to ourselves. Why should I live to myself? What have I ever done or what could I ever do to deserve being the center of my life? But Jesus did far more than we could ever have hoped or imagined. He conquered sin, death and hell for us. Let's live for him!

Jesus, thank you for conquering death for me. I will live for you. Amen.

While they were stoning him, Stephen prayed, "Lord Jesus, receive my spirit." (Acts 7:59)

UNAFRAID OF DEATH

Are we afraid to die? Many people are. We might think that something as important and as certain as death would be thought of and prepared for by everybody. But that is not the case. Many people live their lives trying to forget about death. They put off thinking about death until it stares them in the face.

Stephen wasn't afraid to die. He boldly testified in front of his enemies even though he could see that it was working them up into a murderous rage. Stephen did not carelessly put his life in danger, but he certainly was not going to deny his Savior to save it.

Stephen did not see death as the end of all things but rather as a deliverance, a gateway to heaven and eternal life. On Stephen's lips was also the same confession that the Apostle Paul made, "We are confident, I say, and would prefer to be away from the body and at home with the Lord" (2 Corinthians 5:8). Although death may have caused temporary separation from his fellow Christians on earth, it meant an eternal reunion with his Lord and Savior whom he loved.

This bold disciple was certain of eternal life because he died in the name of the Lord Jesus. Death could not hold Jesus who paid for Stephen's sins, so it would not be able to triumph over him either. The great Apostle Paul mocked the power of death. "Where, O death, is your victory? Where, O death, is your sting? . . . But thanks be to God! He gives us the victory through our Lord Jesus Christ" (1 Corinthians 15:55,57).

Stephen faced death as fearlessly as he faced his enemies. The Lord Jesus had not deserted him in this life. He would not desert him in death either. Meeting his death confident of the Lord's deliverance was the last great triumph of Stephen's faith here on this earth.

We do not have to fear dying any more than Stephen or Paul did. Our Savior has destroyed the fear of death. We are told in the verse following today's text that Stephen fell asleep. That doesn't sound very fearful, does it? Our death also will be a sleep from which our Savior can easily awaken us.

We trust in Jesus as our Savior from sin. Let us also be confident that he will grant us deliverance from death. Believe his promise, "I am the resurrection and the life. He who believes in me will live, even though he dies" (John 11:25).

Lord Jesus, remove all fear of death from me. Help me to see in death a deliverance from this world to be with you forever. Amen.

And if we die, we die to the Lord. (Romans 14:8)

DEATH—THE BEGINNING OF A WHOLE NEW LIFE

Paul's statement, "And if we die, we die to the Lord," like his statement, "If we live, we live to the Lord," expresses an expectation. A Christian is expected to die to the Lord.

But what does that mean, to die to the Lord? It means, first of all, recognizing that the time and place of your dying is not in your hands. That is something which must be left entirely in the hands of the Lord Jesus. The thought, "It's my life, and I can end it if I want," is not the attitude of one seeking to please the Lord.

Dying to the Lord also means willingly accepting the Lord's final summons to leave this world. Dying to the Lord means commending your soul into his care when he calls you from this life. Dying to the Lord means confidently looking forward to being with the Lord forever in the eternal bliss of heaven.

Rather than shrinking away from this expectation stated by Paul, pray God that you are among those of whom it can be said, "They died to the Lord."

Death is the final door through which everyone must pass before entering eternity. For some that door represents the absolute end to everything, beyond which there is nothing. For others, passing through that door is a cause for fear, because it leads to the unknown or because it leads to judgment and condemnation.

Through the example of his resurrection the Lord Jesus demonstrated that death is not the absolute end. Rather it is the beginning of a whole new existence. Through his saving work the Lord Jesus has made it possible for Christians to face the final judgment confident of God's reward rather than his punishment.

Christ Jesus has told his followers that for them the life to come will be a blessed and happy existence. The Lord Jesus has made it possible for believers to face death without fear. To use St. Paul's words, Jesus has made it possible "to die to the Lord."

Blessed are those who die to the Lord! Lord Jesus, strengthen our faith so that we are among them.

With peace and joy I now depart;
God's child I am with all my heart.
I thank thee, death, thou leadest me
To that true life where I would be.
So cleansed by Christ, I fear not death.
Lord Jesus, strengthen Thou my faith. Amen.

23

While they were stoning him, Stephen prayed, "Lord Jesus, receive my spirit." (Acts 7:59)

FAITHFUL TO THE END

"**W**hy? Why did he have to die? He was such a faithful follower of Jesus. He actively served the Lord and was sorely needed by the early church. Why did the Lord take him so soon?"

The questions are familiar to many of us. I'm sure they were familiar to the earliest Christians. When Stephen was stoned to death, he was a highly respected church member. But why did he have to die in such a way and at what appeared to be the prime of his life? The answer is simply: it was God's will. The death of Stephen has remained one of the finest examples of being faithful to the end, and many a Christian has been strengthened by Stephen's example. When he was being murdered, he did not curse the name of Jesus, nor did he voice the question, "Why must I die now, Lord?" Rather, it is written that with his last ounce of courage and faith Stephen confidently prayed: "Lord Jesus, receive my spirit." There was no doubt in his mind. Jesus was his Savior from sin, death and hell.

What an example Stephen is for us! He was faithful to the end. He accepted God's will as good. Even though in this life the will of God occasionally seems hard to understand, we too can continue to find the peace and hope that Stephen found. It is a peace and hope which moved him and can move us to pray at our last hour: "Lord Jesus, receive my spirit."

If you know of someone who is dying, share with him the story of Stephen, for through it God the Holy Spirit offers peace and courage, strength and conviction—offers that same hope of eternal glory which Stephen had in Christ.

Oh, for a faith that will not shrink
Tho' pressed by many a foe;
That will not tremble on the brink
Of poverty or woe;

A faith that keeps the narrow way
Till life's last spark is fled
And with a pure and heavenly ray
Lights up the dying bed.

Lord, give us such a faith as this;
And then, whate'er may come,
We'll taste e'en now the hallowed bliss
Of an eternal home. Amen.

I thank my God every time I remember you. In all my prayers for all of you, I always pray with joy because of your partnership in the gospel from the first day until now, being confident of this, that he who began a good work in you will carry it on to completion until the day of Christ Jesus. (Philippians1:3-6)

WILL I BE A CHRISTIAN WHEN I DIE?

This question frequently suggests itself to those who realize the value of their Christian faith. They've read the warnings in the Bible not to fall from faith. They've tasted the sweetness of sure forgiveness, love and hope which faith possesses. They've memorized the passages which remind them that "by grace are ye saved, through faith . . ." and they know that "without faith it is impossible to please him (God)."

How can I know if I will still have my Christian faith when that last test of death comes my way? Parents sometimes ask about their children, "How can I know that our children, rooted in the Word of God, will remain anchored in it when they leave our home?" Can anyone be sure that he will remain a Christian until his dying day?

If we didn't have Paul's reminder to the Philippians and other emphatic statements of the Scriptures, we might answer, "No one can be sure." If we had to depend upon our own self-discipline, determination and strength of character to keep ourselves in the Christian faith, we'd have to answer, "I don't know if I will stay a Christian."

But we have a more sure foundation for our hope than our self-service efforts. Paul points us to our only source of confidence, "He who began a good work in you." God has called Christians to the faith they possess. God created the Gospel fellowship Paul joyfully recalls. God equipped the Philippian Christians for their faithfulness "from the first day until now." Later in this letter Paul reminds the Philippians that it is "God who works in you to will and to act according to his good purpose" (2:13). And what is that good purpose? That we believe his Gospel and have eternal life! God is going to keep us in the Christian faith. How long?

He "will perform it (the good work of faith which he began) until the day of Jesus Christ." God will not fail nor break his promise. "Faith comes from hearing the message, and the message is heard through the word of Christ." Faith is preserved by that same Word through the power of God. We "are shielded by God's power until the coming of the salvation that is ready to be revealed in the last time" (1 Peter 1:5).

O Father, draw me close to Jesus. Keep me close to him in faith, throughout all the storms of life, through death, forever in him. Amen.

For we know, brothers loved by God, that he has chosen you because our gospel came to you not simply with words, but also with power, with the Holy Spirit and with deep conviction. (1 Thessalonians 1:4,5)

HOW CAN YOU BE SO SURE

"**J**erry, you're sure that you're gong to heaven after you die," the young welder said to his friend across the lunch table. "That's neat! But how can you be so sure? I mean, how can anyone be sure that God has chosen them for heaven?" Paul wrote to the congregation in Thessalonica, "We know that he has chosen you." The obvious question they might have asked was, "How can you be sure?" Paul and his co-workers didn't have God's throne room bugged. They didn't receive golden tablets from an angel with the names of these Christians on them. Yet they could speak with authority and say, "We know."

Paul and the other missionaries based their statement, not on a dream or feelings they had about these people, but on facts that were readily observable. The gospel came to these people "not simply with words" but "with power." The Thessalonians didn't treat the gospel like a fable. They received it as "the power of God for the salvation of everyone who believes" and as the "words of eternal life." The gospel of Jesus Christ changed their lives. They were never the same after they heard it.

Along with the gospel came the Holy Ghost with his gifts of love, joy, peace, patience and kindness. These trademarks of the Holy Spirit were evident in these people. The "deep conviction" these Christians displayed in the face of persecution indicated to the missionaries that they were elect of God. Paul knew that where there was Christian faith, love and hope, there were God's chosen ones. Most of all, Paul was confident that the preaching of the gospel would not be without its effect. For God had promised through the Prophet Isaiah, "My word will not return to me empty, but will accomplish what I desire and achieve the purpose for which I sent it."

If we have one of those days when nothing seems to go right, or if our doctor schedules us for our second major surgery in less than six months, we may not feel very chosen. But thank God, being chosen isn't a matter of feeling. God has verified that he has forgiven us and opened heaven through Christ. That's a fact. The powerful effect that message has had upon our hearts and lives is clearly visible. "The Spirit himself testifies with our spirit that we are God's children."

Holy Spirit, teach me to stop searching for the certainty of salvation within me but rather in my crucified Savior. Amen.

We believe that Jesus died and rose again and so we believe that God will bring with Jesus those who have fallen asleep in him. (1 Thessalonians 4:14)

OUR BLESSED HOPE

In a world that is filled with all sorts of doubts about death and what happens to the body after death, it is understandable that hopelessness and insecurity will mark people's attitudes toward the deaths of those dear to them. God's people will not be unaffected by these attitudes of a world lost in sin.

But if "we believe that Jesus died and rose again," then there is no reason to grieve over our deceased loved ones as those without hope. Thus Paul encouraged the Thessalonians that they might conquer their grief born out of the hopeless views of an unbelieving world. It is the same faith that needs to be firmly established in us to help us bear our grief when death strikes.

To experience hope in the midst of grief, believe in the living Jesus. When Jesus' good friend Lazarus died and his sisters were grief-stricken, Jesus turned their attention to himself. "Your brother will rise again. . . . I am the resurrection and the life. He who believes in me will live, even though he dies; and whoever lives and believes in me will never die."

Anticipate the resurrection when the cloud of death hovers overhead. That is something the Thessalonians did not do, and it's something even Jesus' disciples did not do. One would think the disciples would have been waiting at the grave of Jesus on Easter Sunday for him to come out. Instead they went into hiding when they heard the grave was empty. Though Jesus had told them he would spend no more than three days in the grave and though they had visible proof in the resurrection miracles, the disciples were despondent and without hope in the moment of Jesus' death because they did not anticipate the blessed hope of the resurrection.

Next time we stand at the coffin of a loved one or contemplate our own death, let us not forget our blessed hope. We know most assuredly that those who die in Jesus, God will raise from the dead. And he will bring their souls together with their risen bodies to enjoy the happiness of heaven forever. May our sorrowing hearts be uplifted in this blessed hope!

Lord Jesus, my resurrected Savior, teach me to anticipate with the hope of faith the glorious resurrection of all those who live and die in you. Amen.

He had James, the brother of John, put to death with the sword. (Acts 12:2)

A DEATH THAT BEFITS A CHRISTIAN

How do you want to die? In your sleep? Perhaps you've never thought about it.

Few people would choose to die as James did—beheaded by an executioner. It was not that he had done anything wrong. He was not a criminal. King Herod merely wanted to make a show of killing a Christian to please the people. James was arrested and executed. Thus one of Jesus' closest disciples became the first apostle to suffer martyrdom—to die for his faith. He drank his cup of suffering.

Yet we could wish that all people could die as James did, not in the sense of being executed, but in the sense of being faithful to Christ till death. No amount of tears could change the fact that James died a blessed death. For his death merely opened the door to eternal life in heaven. His death boldly proclaimed to the world that Christians have something worth living for and worth dying for. Death has no hold on Christians. Christ has removed death's sting.

We pray that God would also give us a blessed end. That has nothing to do with the type of death, whether natural, or accidental or violent (though it is certainly proper to pray for a peaceful type of death). Rather we want to have a blessed end in the same sense that James did. We want to approach death with a firm faith in Christ as our Savior. We want the assurance that death will be the entrance to heaven. We want to know that no sin can condemn us, for Christ has suffered for all our sins. Because he lives, we shall live forever with him.

We also pray that our end may be blessed in the sense of it being a bold confession of our faith. As James willingly bowed to the executioner's sword rather than deny Christ, so we pray we may bravely accept whatever end God has in store for us. If others would see us going to our grave complaining, that would not speak well of our faith. But if others see us praising God and voicing our confidence in the eternal life awaiting us, they will be witnessing one of the strongest Christian testimonies we could give.

We don't have to die a martyr's death to have a blessed end. Every Christian who dies believing in Christ as his Savior and confessing his faith in whatever ways are available has just as blessed an end as James. May God give us all such a death.

Lord, keep my faith growing, so I may die as befits a Christian. Amen.

For to me, to live is Christ and to die is gain. (Philippians 1:21)

WITH THE LORD IN LIFE AND DEATH

For me to live is Jesus,
To die is gain for me;
Then, whensoe'er he pleases,
I meet death willingly.

Meet death willingly? Yes. The hymnist could do it. St. Paul could do it. So can we. How? Isn't death something to be feared? Not when we know that death has lost its victory and sting. Not when we know that the Lord has paid for our sins with his death on the cross. Death must no longer be feared, for on the other side of death's door lies the gift of eternal life in heaven for every child of God.

What a glorious place heaven will be! Scripture tells us that in heaven we will personally be with our Savior. We will be his people. God himself will be with us. He will wipe every tear from our eyes. There will be no more death or mourning or crying or pain. The old order of things will have passed away. No wonder St. Paul refers to death as a "gain" for himself in today's text. Forever with the Lord—that is the glorious hope every child of God may have.

But St. Paul could also proclaim, "For to me, to live is Christ." Paul is simply stating that all his living activity is centered in Christ and that Christ controls his life on this earth. The will of the Lord directed Paul's thoughts, words and deeds in this life. St. Paul was totally dedicated to his Savior. By the power of the Holy Spirit Paul was with the Lord, and the Lord was with Paul in life and death.

Will we not also want to be with the Savior in life and in death? Absolutely! Think of his love for us. We have broken God's holy law, but Jesus kept it perfectly in our stead. He credits our account with his perfect holiness. The punishment we deserved for breaking God's law— Jesus has suffered that too in our stead. He died on the cross to pay for our sins. We have not deserved it, but out of the love of his heart he has given us the hope of eternal life in heaven. What love we will want to give our Savior in return! We will want him to guide, control and direct our life on this earth and our life with him in heaven. By the power the Holy Spirit alone can give, we with St. Paul proclaim, "For to me, to live is Christ and to die is gain!"

Take my will and make it thine,
It shall be no longer mine;
Take my heart, it is thine own,
It shall be thy royal throne.
Take my love, my Lord, I pour
At thy feet its treasure-store;
Take myself, and I will be
Ever, only, all, for thee. Amen.

As it is written: "For your sake we face death all day long." (Romans 8:36)

LIVE FOR HIM UNTIL HE CALLS US HOME

She was well along in years. No longer was she able to leave her room or her bed without assistance. Often she felt totally useless. "What am I still good for? Why does the Lord want me to live in this helplessness?"

This is a common feeling among the shut-ins and elderly. They prefer to leave this world as soon as possible. Sometimes they feel resentful toward God himself for still letting them live. What good can their lives bring to them or anyone else? They feel they are a burden on others.

In Paul's time it wasn't so much the fear of old age and the nearness of death for which he counseled the Christians in Rome; it was death by persecution. "We face death all day long." Paul's willingness to suffer all, even death, came because there was another who had done the same for him. In fact, Paul knew the truth that the same man who gave his life for him did so for everyone. This made Paul, who knew how undeserving he was, humbly take on the responsibility of becoming a missionary for the cause of this unselfish man.

The man, of course, was Jesus Christ, the Son of God and the Son of man. Paul's sinfulness could not be put aside by anything he did, but Jesus proved by his resurrection from the dead that he had conquered sin, death and the devil. Jesus substituted his righteousness for the unrighteousness of Paul and all sinners.

The joy of receiving this free gift of salvation set Paul to the task of preaching the message of salvation through Jesus Christ. When we realize Paul's willingness to give even his life for the sake of spreading the good news, it brings shame on those of us who grumble and complain about the situation today.

The shut-ins and elderly who don't know for what reason God has kept them alive must count their blessings under God and realize their purpose as his children. They can smile, for God is with them. They can thank God for food and warmth. They can pray every day thanking God for every gift, asking for his mercy upon them and others and interceding for others who have needs. Their kindness, patience and love—all fruits of faith in their Savior-God—can be a good example to many.

Yes, God has a purpose for all of us here on earth, until he wills to bring us home.

Lord, still use us for heaven's sake. Amen.

30

How great is the love the Father has lavished on us, that we should be called the children of God! And that is what we are! (1 John 3:1)

REMEMBER—YOU ARE GOD'S OWN

Have you ever considered how unusual the love of God for us sinners is? In the original language of the Bible the expression translated "how great" suggests the thought of being foreign. God's love for us sinners is so unusual that we might say it is foreign to our way of thinking and acting.

We would never have thought of, much less carried out, the idea of freeing guilty people by paying the cost of their guilt and then receiving them into our own household. But this is what God has done for us.

The fact that we are sons and daughters in God's family is not something to be taken for granted. It is a gracious gift from God, and it ought to fill our hearts and minds with wonder. Just think of it. God calls us son or daughter! He is calling us his very own.

Of course, it would be one thing to be called a son or a daughter and then have the facts reveal that what we are called and what we actually are happen to be two different things. For example, people may call you a "tightwad" when in reality you are quite generous. On the other hand when God calls us "children," that is exactly what we are. God doesn't give us an empty title. His Word is truth. It always means what it says and says what it means. So when God says we are his "children," he really means it.

The reason this is so hard to believe is because this is not natural to us. We are by nature corrupt and sinful, enemies of God. Only by his grace have we been renewed. God doesn't just talk about this; he takes action! His love moves him to action. He "lavishes" his love on us by making us his people.

What a wonderful way to begin each day! What a wonderful way to close each day! I am God's own. He made me his own and he keeps me as his own.

Dear Lord, we stand in awe of your love for us. It is too wonderful for us to comprehend, but we praise and thank you for it. Strengthen us in the confidence and the comfort of knowing that we are your people. Help us also to act like we are yours. Bless our lives as our effective witness to the power of your love and grace. Amen.

But you received the Spirit of sonship. And by him we cry, "Abba, Father."(Romans 8:15)

CHILDREN IN A LOVING RELATIONSHIP

It starts with the first "ma-ma, da-da." It grows into messages like "Hi, Mom! Hi, Dad!" It is a relationship of love between parents and children. The simple words bring a feeling of joy and warmth to the hearts of mothers and fathers everywhere. By voicing them, children show that they regard their parents as friends, not foes, as partners in the process of living and not adversaries.

It takes work to build up that kind of spirit in a human family. Trust and confidence, acceptance and forgiveness must be mutually exchanged. That is not to say that parents shouldn't be parents. For the benefit of all, there must be order and authority. There must be a head of the family who finalizes decisions. And children know that. They need it and want it.

God's children in his spiritual family of faith recognize that also. They know that God is still God. To us, he is not just a "spiritual pal." He is still in control; his will is still the last word. He is deserving of honor and respect to the utmost degree.

But there is a relationship of love between us and our heavenly Father which pervades our entire being. He is the one who chose to make us his children through his Spirit. He is the one who took action to adopt us into his family. He is the one who sent our Redeemer to give us the robe of righteousness. He is the one who stands at the gate eager to welcome us prodigals back home.

Is it any wonder that we delight in calling him by that familiar, but meaningful term "Father"? In that loving relationship is embodied some marvelous blessings and privileges.

First, there is the privilege of talking with him as a true friend. Every day, in every circumstance, we can place our hand in his through prayer. We can place upon him our perplexity, our problems, our sorrow, our woe and our worry.

Then there is peaceful confidence. It is the trust that our Father will not give us a stone when what we really need is bread. It is the serenity that comes from knowing that he makes all things—yes, all—work for our benefit.

Finally, there is his abiding presence; we are never out of his care or concern. We are never at a loss for someone stronger or wiser. He is our Father.

Keep me, Father, as your dear child, now and forever. Amen.

We share in his sufferings in order that we may also share in his glory. (Romans 8:17)

CHILDREN FOR AN ETERNITY OF GLORY

Children have remarkable impatience. "How much farther, Dad?" "How much longer, Mom?" "Can we do it right away?" All are common childhood questions. It's only as we get older that we realize time goes fast enough as it is. "Don't wish your life away" is the oft-voiced advice from the older generation to the younger.

In a sense, we children of God never really grow up. We also are numbered among those who just can't wait. We live in eager anticipation of what is to come in eternity. Right now our existence is all tied up in the progressive ploddings of everyday life, much as school children bear the Monday to Friday schedule in anticipation of the coming weekend.

It is not so much unhappiness with the present situation that keeps us going as it is the anticipation for the future. In fact, it is the expectation, no, the certainty of a better future which makes the present bearable.

Children of God certainly have happy, joyful and satisfying moments in this earthly life. The enjoyment of God's gracious blessings in family and friends, possessions and activities is pleasing to them. But they don't last. They change, rust and disappear. Even on the brightest day, there is always a gray cloud. The weekend is always followed by Monday morning.

Yet we know the time is coming when things are not only going to get better; they are going to become perfect. And they are going to stay that way. There will be a fullness of joy, without any trouble spot to diminish it. There will be happiness forever, without any passage of time to detract from it. There will be radiant, glorious bodies and souls, without any tears or tribulations to trouble them.

For the child of God, the prospect of an eternity of glory shared with our Savior is the light at the end of the tunnel. Our Spirit-wrought faith has so united us with Christ that we share everything: the blessings of his redemptive work, the cross of suffering in this world—but as the ultimate—the glory which he already enjoys.

Pretty hard to wait for that, isn't it? Pretty difficult to be patient when it seems so long and so far. But it's just that remarkable impatience which marks us as CHILDREN IN GOD'S FAMILY.

Lord, give me patience, both to deal with the sorrows of this life and to wait for the day of sorrowless glory. Amen.

Our citizenship is in heaven. (Philippians 3:20)

CHILDREN OF GOD—CITIZENS OF HEAVEN

"Citizens of heaven" is more than a pious phrase that has a pleasing sound. It is descriptive of the great honor which God is pleased to bestow on us for Jesus' sake. Citizenship in Israel was highly prized in Old Testament times. Roman citizenship was highly prized in New Testament times. American citizenship is highly prized in our day. But how can we ever begin to compare any of these with citizenship in heaven?

The kingdoms of this world come to an end. They are constantly vulnerable. Citizens of this world have to switch allegiance as their rulers and governments change. Earthly citizenship is never sure, and its eventual loss is inevitable. But the citizen of heaven belongs to a kingdom that will never end and never change. It stands firm and sure, for Jesus is defending it and those in it. The citizen of heaven will not have his citizenship taken from him, nor will his citizenship end when he dies. He has an "inheritance that can never perish, spoil or fade—kept in heaven" (1 Peter 1:4).

The heart of the blessing of citizenship in heaven is that its citizens are the redeemed people of God. They are the people to whom God has granted his mercy in Jesus Christ. They are people who have been delivered from the condemnation and destruction which will belong to the enemies of God. Rather than being separated from God as foreigners and strangers, because of Christ we have become fellow citizens with the saints and members of his family.

We ought to prize our citizenship highly. It is not something man can achieve or merit by his own efforts, but it is a citizenship awarded by the grace of God. We are citizens of heaven because Jesus won a place for us there by his atoning death on the cross. He sealed our citizenship in heaven by his resurrection from the dead. And he ascended into heaven to prepare a place for us there.

Through the gospel invitation the Holy Spirit led us to believe these wonderful truths concerning Christ. By the powerful promises of God in the Scriptures, we are assured that we belong to Christ and that heaven belongs to us. Men may steal our earthly life. But no one, no, nothing, can separate us from the love of God in Christ or deprive us of our citizenship in heaven.

We thank you, O Lord, that you have called us into your kingdom of grace and mercy. We rejoice that you have forgiven our sins and written our names in the Book of Life. Amen.

Our citizenship is in heaven. (Philippians 3:20)

CHILDREN OF GOD—LOOK FORWARD

During his lifetime Abraham lived in tents and led his herds across Canaan. He had no permanent home, nor did he own any land except for the family burial plot. He was a stranger, a foreigner, in the land in which he lived. Nevertheless, God promised him that one day his descendants would call the whole land of Canaan their possession and their home.

Citizens of heaven are also strangers and outsiders in this world. Here we have no lasting home. Indeed, we are warned not to make too much of the things of this world nor to set our hearts upon them. For we have been promised an inheritance far richer and better than anything in this world. As believers in Christ and citizens of heaven, we will have a new heaven and a new earth for our home. We walk now on streets of earth or of stone, but then we shall walk on streets of gold through gates of pearl in the Paradise of God.

We look forward to our homecoming. Each day here brings us one day closer to it. Still we have to be on our guard. For each day also threatens to overwhelm us with its cares and temptations. But we are not alone. Our Lord Jesus is present with us in his word and sacraments. He assures and reassures us that our sins have been forgiven, that we are the children of God, and that our names have been written in the Book of Life. Each day we can turn to his word for strength and encouragement. Each day through that word he leads our thoughts heavenward and shows us how we are to live as citizens of heaven.

Without the word of God we would soon become discouraged and lose our way. But with its message in our hearts, we are encouraged to look forward and to sing:

My walk is heavenward all the way;
Await, my soul, the morrow,
When thou shalt find release for aye
From all thy sin and sorrow.
All worldly pomp, begone!
To heaven I now press on.
For all the world I would not stay;
My walk is heavenward all the way.

Bless the days of our lives, O Lord, that each day may indeed bring us closer to heaven. Forgive us our sins, and guide us on our way. Help us to appreciate the fact of our heavenly citizenship and to rejoice in your salvation. Amen.

Brothers, think of what you were when you were called. (1 Corinthians 1:26)

CHILDREN OF GOD—REJOICE!

The past can bring to mind sorrows or joys. The painful memories of immorality, materialism and idolatry brought sorrow to the minds of Christians in Corinth as they remembered the way they were. They realized how far they were from what God wants his people to be. Like sheep that had gone astray, they were once helplessly and hopelessly lost in the depths of sin. What a sorrowful state to be in!

Their reminiscing was to be also the source of rejoicing. For Paul reminded them that they were "called." That brings to mind the amazing grace of God, who calls people to be his own. That call is even more wondrous when one realizes that God has called people who aren't worthy of his call. God "has saved us and called us to a holy life—not because of anything we have done but because of his own purpose and grace [which] was given us in Christ Jesus" (2 Timothy 1:9).

Our membership in God's family depends on his action for us and in us as the Holy Spirit touches our hearts through the word. God alone stands at center stage with the spotlight shining on his grace revealed brilliantly at the cross of Christ. Remembering what we are in the light of what we were brings joy in Christ to the hearts of God's people. With rejoicing God's people confess that "Jesus Christ . . . has redeemed me, a lost and condemned creature, purchased and won me from all sins, from death and from the power of the devil, not with gold or silver, but with his holy, precious blood and with his innocent suffering and death."

We were "made alive with Christ even when we were dead in transgressions" (Ephesians 2:5). Indeed, we are special people by the grace of God, who loves us with an everlasting love.

All that I was, my sin, my guilt,
My death was all mine own;
All that I am I owe to thee,
My gracious God, alone.
Thy Word first made me feel my sin,
It taught me to believe;
Then, in believing, peace I found,
And now I live, I live!

All that I am, e'en here on earth,
All that I hope to be,
When Jesus comes and glory dawns,
I owe it, Lord, to Thee. Amen.

How great is the love the Father has lavished on us, that we should be called children of God! (1 John 3:1)

CHILDREN OF GOD—LOVED BY THE FATHER

A teacher once asked her pupils what was most amazing about God. A child responded, "He knows all about me, and yet he still loves me." Indeed, God's love for us is amazing. He does know all about us. He knows about our defying his commandments, our failing to carry out his will, our unloving thoughts and unkind words. He knows we deserve nothing but his wrath. Yet, he still loves us. He loves us so much that he was willing to send his Son to die for our sins.

In our text, John tells us that the Father has lavished his love on us. God loves us very dearly. In fact, we could say that his love for us is so vast that we cannot even begin to measure it.

The fact that we are God's children tells us that God has lavished his love on us. We do not deserve to be God's children. We forfeited this privilege because of our sins. Yet God in his love for us satisfied his justice. He made us acceptable to himself. He brought us to faith in Jesus. Through faith we possess Christ's righteousness. We stand before God acceptable to him through his Son. We are God's sons and daughters. We will inherit the heavenly kingdom our Father has prepared for us.

What a comfort it is to know God loves us. There are times when our conscience condemns us. We recognize our sinfulness and wonder how God can let us into heaven. When problems arise, we may feel God doesn't care about us anymore. At times such as these we need to look beyond our feelings and reason. By faith we lay hold of the words and promises of God. It is not how we feel about God that gives us comfort. The fact that God loves us gives us hope.

"How great is the love the Father has lavished on us, that we should be called children of God!" What a joy it is to bask in the radiance of these words. We are sinners, it is true. We deserve nothing but God's wrath. Yet, God loves us. Christ paid for our sins. We are God's children. Heaven is ours. This is a fact. Thank God for that!

Was it for crimes that I had done
He groaned upon the tree?
Amazing pity, grace unknown,
And love beyond degree!

God made him who had no sin to be sin for us, so that in him we might become the righteousness of God. (2 Corinthians 5:21)

CHILDREN OF GOD—SAINTS

Jesus had no sin. He was born without sin and he lived without sin. When he was put on trial, he was declared innocent of all charges by Pontius Pilate. God the Father also had declared him to be innocent when he said from heaven: "This is my Son whom I love, whom I have chosen; with him I am well pleased."

For us, God made him to be sin. He charged the sins of all mankind against Jesus. He suffered the curse of sin and endured its just punishment. This is one part of the great exchange. God took the guilt of all the world and laid it on his own sinless Son.

The other part of this great exchange is that the perfect holiness of Jesus is ours by faith. In Christ we have a new and perfect righteousness. It is a holiness just as genuine as the sinless life of Christ. It is a holiness which God himself accepts as perfect; after all, it comes from him. We are saints. That's what God has made us, and that's how God treats us because of what Jesus has done.

The righteousness that is ours by faith in Christ is complete. It doesn't need additives or any final touches. It's not like instant coffee or soup where you need to add water. It's compared in the Bible to a garment that's already sewn and ready to wear. By faith we put it on and we appear before God looking beautifully and impeccably dressed.

Let's remember this when we feel depressed. This perfect righteousness takes away our guilt and our fears. It takes away our tendencies to look at ourselves as mere faces lost in the crowd, run-of-the-mill human beings. We're saints. God made us holy; God treats us as though we had never sinned. That makes our life a brand new life in Christ.

The more we can see ourselves as God sees us, the more we will grow in our own personal holiness as well. I'm a child of God, a saint. I'm not going to follow any and everyone who invites me or encourages me to play in the garbage of sin. My brand new, sparkling white robe of righteousness in Christ makes me want to stay far away from the dirt.

**Jesus, thy blood and righteousness
My beauty are, my glorious dress;
Midst flaming worlds, in these arrayed,
With joy shall I lift up my head. Amen.**

The Spirit himself testifies with our spirit that we are God's children. (Romans 8:16)

CHILDREN WITH PERFECT SECURITY

Have you ever been in a group where you felt you really didn't belong? Not just because you shouldn't have been there, but because you just didn't feel part of the group? Because everyone else knew one another and you were the stranger? Because you had nothing in common with the rest of the crowd? Uncomfortable, uneasy, uncertain, unsure?

Sometimes we are also more than a bit uncertain about our relationship within the family of God. The devil uses our doubts and our worries, our sins and our weaknesses, to lead us to ask, "Do I really belong? Am I really one of God's children? Is he really my loving, caring heavenly Father? Or am I just deluding myself into thinking that all is well?"

So much of what we do and say in our everyday lives is tied up in those emotions we call our "feelings." And in normal conditions, our feelings can well be a barometer of what's going on inside of us. We may accurately read the signs of the party crowd around us, and then say, "I feel I'm not really wanted; I don't really belong."

It would be easy to make the mistake of carrying over this emphasis on feelings into our spiritual lives. We could get the impression that you must "feel saved" in order to be saved. Oh, yes, at the high points of our Christian lives, maybe Christmas or Easter, we feel pretty faith-filled. But all too often our faith is weak, questions are unanswered, doubts prevail, not-so-notable sins plague the conscience, and our spirit fades and fails. We feel, "Am I really wanted? Do I really belong to God's family?"

God's children, however, have a vital and eternally true assurance. It comes not from within us, but from outside of us. It is not based on how we feel, but on how God feels; his Spirit speaks to us in a thousand places in the written Word. Over and over again he says: "You may feel unlovable, but I love you. You may feel you are an outcast, but I have adopted you to be my child."

It is just when we have those weak and failing feelings that we are invited to come back to him through his Word. To perk up your spirit, let his Spirit speak. You'll be blessed with the perfect security of knowing, "I really belong."

O Lord, give me your Spirit so that by your Word of promise I may trust that I am truly one of your children. Amen.

And you also are among those who are called to belong to Jesus Christ. (Romans 1:6)

CHILDREN OF GOD—WANTED BY THE FATHER

Some of you may remember those words jumping out at you during World War II from a poster. Our government, caricatured in the figure of Uncle Sam, pointed a demanding finger in our direction and implied that we were needed and had an obligation to fulfill. "I want you," said the poster.

One of the greatest of human needs is just that, the need to feel wanted. We need to be assured someone cares for us, and we are important to that person. Yet there are many dark times in our lives when we lose touch with those who hold us near and dear. Sometimes it is because they have moved away from us, literally and figuratively. More often it is because we have lost our perspective.

During the depression of the 1930s a lecturer spoke to a businessmen's group. He took a sheet of white paper, pinned it to the wall, then with a pencil put a black spot in the middle of the paper.

He asked, "What do you see?"

A man in the front row squinted and said, "A black spot."

Then the speaker said, "That's the trouble with us. We see the black spot, and we fail to see the great white field of opportunity surrounding it."

When the twelve spies went to survey the promised land of Canaan, ten of them saw only the walled cities and the giants. Two, Caleb and Joshua, saw the grapes and the pomegranates, the milk and honey.

So often in life, even though we have been called by the gospel to belong to the family of God, we fail to see the great blessings we have in that family. We see only the black spot of sorrow, of suffering, of work, of aggravation, of trouble. We see the walls and mountains of life, which seem so unscalable, the giants of opposition and difficulty. Focusing on the dark spots, we lose sight of the great white area of God's boundless love. We miss the fruit, the milk and honey of peace, pleasure and power that God has set before us.

Having entered God's family through faith in Christ, let us accept the blessings he sends us as evidence of the Father's love. Christ has made us God's children and we rejoice over every gift that comes from our Father's hand. For with each new blessing our heavenly Father reminds us, "I want you!" Keeping that thought uppermost in our minds will help us to focus not on the little black spot but on the glorious expanse of God's love.

Lord, keep reminding us how much you care for us and want us. Amen.

Pray continually; give thanks in all circumstances, for this is God's will for you in Christ Jesus. (1 Thessalonians 5:17,18)

OUR PRAYERS—COMPLAINTS OR THANKSGIVING?

The snowplow came around the corner, and with a giant "swoosh" the entrance to the driveway was blocked with wet, sticky snow from the street. Tommy and his father had shoveled the heavy stuff for over an hour, and now it was like starting all over again.

Impatiently Tommy demanded, "Why did God make this snow so heavy? Why couldn't it be the light fluffy kind?"

"If that were the case," said Tommy's father, "you'd be missing something. Look around you. This snow sticks to the trees. It's like God has begun decorating for Christmas. And it packs really well—just right for making a snowman."

That night during the family prayer everyone was surprised to hear Tommy pray, "Thank you, God, for heavy snow."

We are all a little like Tommy, aren't we? We often tend to dwell so much on the negative side of things that we fail to see God's goodness working in our lives. Our old Adam is a true pessimist. He even changes good encouragements from our Lord, like "pray continually," into hopelessly heavy burdens.

There is a way, however, to keep our sinful pessimism in check. It's to think like a saint and not like a sinner. It's to let God's positive promises outweigh our negative doubts. It's to have faith that a gracious God, who loves us in Jesus Christ, "in all things works for the good of those who love him."

That's right. In all things God works for our good. Even when it looks bad, it will turn out for good. The bloodstained cross and the empty tomb prove that.

Therefore Paul can say, "Give thanks in all circumstances." That's one way of following the encouragement to "pray continually." Simply change the complaint list into a thanksgiving list. It's bound to result in more of our thoughts rising to our Father's throne.

Positive, praying faith comes in only one way—by having God continually remind us that we are "in Christ Jesus." We are in his family through Christ, and he as our Father is eager to listen.

Wait for your Savior by praying — praying continually. Thank God for your "heavy snow." Even the burdens he sends are for our good.

Dear Father, teach us to thank you for all things. Even under life's burdens may your love draw us closer to the Savior, whom we eagerly await. In his name we pray. Amen.

Do not be anxious about anything, but in everything, by prayer and petition, with thanksgiving, present your requests to God. (Philippians 4:6)

PRAYER—SOLUTION FOR WORRY

Have you ever found yourself sitting in a hospital waiting room, anticipating a doctor's report on a biopsy? Those are anxious moments to be sure. You think of Paul's words: "Do not be anxious about anything." You believe those words, but that doesn't make it any easier to practice them, or so it seems anyway. "Do not be anxious about anything" doesn't mean to be foolhardy, but rather, don't be bothered or troubled.

Now the doctor may tell you not to worry about your condition, but you can't just tune out your problem and forget about it. It just doesn't happen that easily. You can try all kinds of things to get your mind off that biopsy report, but it doesn't go away by itself. You can deaden the pain, or superficially or artificially block out the tension, but that won't remove the cause of the problem.

Paul has a genuine solution for worry-free joy—PRAYER. One of our hymns tells us:

Oh, what peace we often forfeit,
Oh, what needless pain we bear,

All because we do not carry
Everything to God in prayer.

And isn't that true? St. Peter writes, "Cast all your anxiety on him because he cares for you." Getting rid of our worries before they worry us—that would be real joy.

And that is exactly what Paul suggests, "But in everything by prayer and petition, with thanksgiving, present your requests to God." Certainly God knows our needs even before we ask, yet he wants us to ask and promises to answer our prayers. James tells us in his Epistle, "You do not have because you do not ask God."

Our requests are to be made known to the Lord. In what better hands can any troubles or needs rest than in the hands of God! That's the way to beat worry. Paul's words contain the assurance that God will attend to all we ask or even think. And don't forget, this is done with thanksgiving. Our thanks will naturally be included in our prayers. A thankful heart is also a joyful heart.

Heavenly Father, remind us often to bring our cares to you. Help us to find joy in the assurance of your gracious help. Amen.

Now to him who is able to do immeasurably more than all we ask or imagine, according to his power that is at work within us, to him be glory in the church and in Christ Jesus throughout all generations, for ever and ever! Amen. (Ephesians 3:20,21)

STORM THE GATES OF HEAVEN WITH YOUR PRAYERS

When Samuel Morse invented the telegraph and proceeded to demonstrate the device on a test line that was strung between Washington's Capitol Building and Baltimore, the message he sent over the wires was "What God hath wrought!" It was a "miracle of communications." Man suddenly found himself able to send information across many miles with the speed of electricity.

Even more reason do we Christians have to marvel at the wondrous things that God has wrought for us spiritually and to praise him for them. God sent his Son to deliver us from death and hell. And he sent his Holy Spirit to work that faith in our hearts by which we apprehend our salvation. What a miracle God has wrought—a miracle even greater than that which God did when he parted the Red Sea or when he caused the sun to stand still in the sky.

Having reminded the "saints" at Ephesus of all that God had done for them, Paul closes this section of his letter with a stirring song of praise. In it he glorifies God for his power to do exceedingly more than we ask or think. Because of what God has wrought, and because of what he will continue to do through Christ until the end of time, all glory belongs to him alone.

What an incentive Paul's words are for Christians today! They are an incentive to "think big" when it comes to asking things of the Lord. We have a great and powerful God, who is able to deliver us from every evil and to preserve us unto his heavenly kingdom. We have a Lord who time and time again has demonstrated that he "is able to do immeasurably more than all we ask or imagine." We have a God who also invites us to come to him with all the boldness and confidence of a little child approaching his father.

Maybe you have a particular sin that keeps popping up, one that you find extremely difficult to overcome. It seems that with that sin Satan has found the chink in your armor Should you despair? No! Rather, repent and believe that God has forgiven your sins for Jesus' sake. Storm the gates of heaven with petitions for help to improve your behavior. And know that your heavenly Father, who wants you to ask for deliverance from temptation, will surely answer your pleas and permit you to marvel at "what God hath wrought."

Dear Lord Jesus, increase our trust and confidence in you. Amen.

**Three times I pleaded with the Lord to take it away from me.
(2 Corinthians 12:8)**

TAKE IT TO THE LORD IN PRAYER

"Call upon me in the day of trouble; I will deliver you, and you will honor me." What a tremendously reassuring invitation and promise we have in this psalm verse. And what a comfort it is to us when life turns sour and we are overwhelmed with problems for which there seems to be no earthly relief. This is an invitation and a promise that comes from one who not only sees our troubles but has the power to do something about them. This is almighty God speaking by whose "word the heavens were made; who spoke, and it came to be; who commanded, and it stood firm," with whom nothing is impossible. This is the Lord who is in control of the universe, and certainly in control of our lives. His almighty power knows no limits.

But we pray not only to a God of might and power; we pray also to a God of love and mercy, of goodness and deep concern for our well-being. It was his unsurpassed love for the sinner that moved him to give his one and only Son as the atoning sacrifice for our sins. So Paul exclaimed, "He who did not spare his own Son, but gave him up for us all —how will he not also, along with him, graciously give us all things?" His love is not withdrawn in our tribulation. God's Son suffered affliction in greater degree than any human being has been called upon to endure, yet in that affliction he remained his Father's Son, the object of his love. There is his promise to us all, "For a brief moment I abandoned you, but with deep compassion I will bring you back. . . . I hid my face from you for a moment, but with everlasting kindness I will have compassion on you."

It is also a God of wisdom to whom we pray. He always knows what is best for us, far better than we ourselves know. We can always trust in him to deal with us according to his wise counsel.

The Apostle Paul didn't really have to think about what he should do about the "thorn in his flesh." There was no doubt in his mind about God's ability to heal him. There was no question about his Lord's love for him. He had confidence in the absolute wisdom of God. He pleaded with God, not once, but three times, to take his affliction away.

Calling upon God in our troubles is not a last resort—something we do when we have exhausted all other sources of help. No, it is the first thing we do.

Heavenly Father, we bless you for the privilege of prayer. Amen.

. . . Having been kept by the Holy Spirit from preaching the word in the province of Asia. When they came to the border of Mysia, they tried to enter Bithynia, but the Spirit of Jesus would not allow them to. (Acts 16:6,7)

GOD'S NO!

Mark Twain once said, "Most people are bothered by those passages in Scripture which they cannot understand; but I always noticed that the passages which troubled me most are those which I do understand." We all get his point, but the fact remains that the ways of God can be a little hard to understand sometimes. Our text for today gives us a good example of that.

Paul had been called by God to preach the gospel to the Gentiles. But when he wanted to minister to the people in Asia, God said, "No." When he wanted to enter Bithynia, God said, "No." It just didn't make any sense to Paul. It must have been a very frustrating experience.

But life is often like that. God warned us about this too when he said through the prophet Isaiah, "For my thoughts are not your thoughts, neither are your ways my ways."

There is only One who is omniscient, and that is God. He operates with a wisdom that is far greater than ours. He never makes mistakes in the ways that he deals with his children. Our text once again serves as a good example of that.

God had a good reason for saying No to Paul and not allowing him to enter Asia or Bithynia at this time. There was a more urgent need in Macedonia. There was a field white for the harvest that required his immediate attention. Once Paul started working there, he understood full well why God had said No to him earlier.

Unfortunately it doesn't always work out that way. There are times we cannot understand why God says No to us. Our loved one is stricken with an incurable disease. We pray with all the confidence we can muster that God will perform a miracle and heal that person. But the answer that comes back to us is No, and we end up shedding our tears at the funeral.

That could be a very bitter pill to swallow. It could fill our hearts with all sorts of doubts about the love of God for us. But when we think of Jesus Christ nailed to the cross and dying for our sins, how can we possibly doubt his love for us? Blessed with wisdom from above, we will continue to put our trust in God even when we can't understand when he says, "No."

O Lord, we believe; help to overcome our unbelief. Amen.

Always giving thanks to God the Father for everything, in the name of our Lord Jesus Christ. (Ephesians 5:20)

GIVE THANKS FOR EVERYTHING

Isn't Paul going a bit far when he encourages the Ephesian Christians—and us as well—to give thanks to God "always"? How can anyone always be thankful? Thankful for loss of a job? Thankful for crop failure? Thankful for the accident that happened on the way to work?

"Yes," Paul adds emphatically, "for everything." Everything? Even for that chronic illness which hinders my effectiveness at work, which is a burden to others, which I ask God frequently and fervently to take away? "Yes, for that too," is Paul's reply.

"But what did I ever do to deserve having all these things go against me?" Paul reminds us that he also "was given a thorn in the flesh." He pleaded with the Lord to take it away. The Lord answered Paul's prayer by showing him that in human weakness God's power would prevail. God's grace was sufficient for all things. To realize that truth was more important than anything else. It brought Paul closer to God than ever before.

That is why Paul reminds us here that "God the Father," is the source of every good and perfect gift. We are to thank him "in the name of our Lord Jesus Christ," who became poor, so that we through his poverty might become rich.

We sinners deserve nothing. Because of our many sins a just God has every right to banish us forever from his holy presence. But this same God in his love took pity on us and gave his only Son as a sacrifice for our sins so that we might live with him forever in heaven.

Knowing this, we also "know that in all things God works for the good of those who love him" and that nothing "in all creation will be able to separate us from the love of God that is in Christ Jesus our Lord" (Romans 8:38,39). No, not even those things that seem to be great misfortunes. We can always give thanks to God for everything!

We see how the wise Christian is, above all, the thankful Christian. The Spirit of thankfulness is the basis for his attitude toward all things in life, also those which bring despair to others. It determines his relationship with his God. It influences his actions toward others. It gives him courage to face problems in spite of disappointments and gives him everlasting hope in the face of death.

Lord, help me always to give thanks for everything. Amen.

Cast all your anxiety on him because he cares for you. (1 Peter 5:7)

CAST ALL YOUR CARE ON HIM IN PRAYER

"**D**on't worry!" That's easy to say. But what if you're taking off down the runway on your first airplane trip or facing the first day on a new job or visiting a doctor for a crucial examination? The human tendency is to fill your mind with anxious thoughts. Yet Peter's counsel to us is: "Don't worry!"

Every care and worry we have, every possible anxiety, can be cast on our gracious Father in heaven. Thus it is foolish for Christians to worry. Peter had experienced this on the Sea of Galilee. When worried about high waves that swamped his boat, he and the other disciples had called out, "Lord, save us!" And Jesus calmed the troubled sea as well as their troubled minds. When he was sinking in the turbulent waves of that same sea, Peter experienced the strong and gracious hand of the Lord, lifting him out of danger.

The Lord invites us to cast all our anxiety on him. But in our human weakness we sometimes insist on clinging to some of these cares. We try to work out by ourselves, or sometimes with another's help, such things as illness, financial difficulty, problems at school, approaching old age, etc. When we insist on carrying some of these burdens ourselves, we forget that the Lord has volunteered to care for us in every need.

In his Sermon on the Mount Jesus cautions us, "Therefore do not worry about tomorrow, for tomorrow will worry about itself. Each day has enough trouble of its own." We are to take one day at a time and rely on the Lord for sufficient strength to see us through that day and entrust the future to his gracious wisdom.

Peter's piece of divine counsel for today is a gracious invitation to pray to God and at the same time a promise that God will hear and answer our prayers. Why worry, when you can pray? We who have learned to know God as a loving father ought to cast our anxieties on him in prayer.

We have a God who cares about us so much that he allowed his own Son to shed his lifeblood to atone for our sins. God cares. He cares about our spiritual needs, and he also cares about our physical needs. We ought to trust steadfastly in his gracious care.

I am trusting Thee, Lord Jesus;
Never let me fall.
I am trusting Thee forever
And for all. Amen.

Because you are sons, God sent the Spirit of his Son into our hearts, the Spirit who calls out, "*Abba*, Father." (Galatians 4:6)

YOU CAN NEVER CALL TOO OFTEN

"**G**ive a gift that keeps on giving." That's how years ago a large company urged its customers to buy its appliances. It was a catchy slogan. And it made sense to a lot of people. Why buy flowers that soon die, while a blender, iron or toaster could be used day after day. But the truth of the matter is many of us have thrown some of those electrical appliances into the trash. Eventually they gave out and stopped giving.

But our heavenly Father gave us the gift which keeps on giving. Jesus our Redeemer made it possible for us to be adopted into God's family. God then "sent the Spirit of his Son into our hearts, the Spirit who calls out, 'Abba, Father.' " Hebrew children called their fathers "Abba," as American children might call their father "Dad" or "Daddy." With the Holy Spirit in our hearts, we Christians have the continuous assurance that God is our Father and we are his children. And so the Holy Spirit in our hearts teaches us to pray, "Abba, Father."

"*Abba*, I need a drink of water," the Hebrew child might call out at night, fully confident that his loving father would answer his request. "*Abba*, hold my hand," the frightened child might say when he needed the firm and loving clasp of his father's hand. Such comfort and confidence belong to every redeemed child of our heavenly Father every day. When the Apostle John thought about this he exclaimed, "How great is the love the Father has lavished on us, that we should be called children of God! And that is what we are!"

What a difference our Redeemer makes in everyday life! If today you face all kinds of anxiety at work, remember Abba. If school days are difficult, you aren't alone. Abba cares. If there are family problems that don't seem to get better, Abba is near. If you are alone, if you are ill, if you need any reassurance today at all, call to Abba. You can never call too often. You can never ask too much. The Father sent us his Son so that he might keep on giving us his love.

**I have called Thee Abba, Father!
I have stayed my heart on Thee.
Storms may howl, and clouds may gather,
All must work for good to me. Amen.**

Cast all your anxiety on him because he cares for you. (1 Peter 5:7)

YOU CAN NEVER ASK TOO MUCH

Everyone has his problems. Until we get to know someone quite well, we may not be aware of his worries and concerns. But we may be sure that he has them hidden away somewhere. A completely carefree life is perhaps never found in this vale of tears. Sin and God's chastening curse upon a sinful world have sown thorns and thistles in everyone's life.

Some of our problems are easily solved. Others are solved with great difficulty. Still others can not be solved at all. It is this last group that brings frustration, fear and unspeakable woe into our lives. As nagging worries, they lodge in our souls and allow us no peace. When they do not occupy our full attention, they churn about in the back of our minds.

Some well-meaning people recommend that we forget our woes. That is easier said than done.

St. Peter has better advice, and he speaks by the Holy Spirit. He says, "Throw your worries on God."

There are two good reasons for heeding his advice. Peter mentions one of them when he says, "He cares for you." While some people care about us more or less, and others, as we say, "couldn't care less," God cares. The other reason for handing our problems over to God is that God is able to cope with difficulties that are too much for us. With God all things are possible.

But Peter has mentioned the reason that is more important for our consideration. It is the one we are most apt to forget. We get caught up in the gloom of our own sinfulness and find it hard to imagine that God could really care about us. That he takes a personal and powerful interest in our woes is almost too much to believe.

Let's take another look at our God. His care for us is so genuine and complete, so wholehearted and sincere, that he gave his only-begotten Son for us, delivering him up to death for our sins. Then he raised him again from the dead, so that we might be sure that Jesus' sacrifice was acceptable. And Jesus himself has promised to come again and to receive us to himself.

Such Good News contradicts all doubt about God's concern for us. God loves me with his whole, infinite Being. He invites me to unload my worries on him. Yes, he commands me to do so, and it is only right that I do.

Lord God, to Thee my ways belong,
Take fear and care away;
Place in my heart salvation's song—
Thy mercy's bright, strong ray. Amen.

I always thank God for you because of his grace given you in Christ Jesus. (1 Corinthians 1:4)

ALWAYS THANKFUL FOR GRACE

Learning to say "Thank you" is an important step in growing up. Learning to thank God, to see and appreciate his grace, is important in growing as a Christian.

The Apostle Paul gave thanks for the grace God gave to the church at Corinth. But if you read further in this letter to Corinth, this thankful praise seems surprising. Serious problems had occurred in this church. The people had fallen into quarreling, immorality, drunkenness and envy. How could Paul always thank God for Christians like those?

Paul hadn't closed his eyes to their sin. As their shepherd, he gave them stern warnings to change their attitude and ways. Yet Paul was sincere in his thankful praise. The grace God had given them in Christ Jesus was the key to Paul's thankfulness. He knew that this love of God had triumphed over sin—even for those Christians at Corinth. In his own life Paul had seen how grace can change a blaspheming enemy of the church into a faithful servant of God.

Grace is the key to new life and thankfulness to God for us also. No one is without sin. God's holy law condemns us all as sinners. But thank God for his grace! He judges each one of us to be righteous and innocent because of what his Son has done for us. Jesus' holy life and sacrifice for us will always be the breath of life for our souls. His work as our Savior is the sure promise of peace with him forever.

Can we really always be thankful for what God does? The Bible shows us God's great love. He is our Savior and the source of everything good in our lives. He guides all the events of history as well as each moment of our day to serve our best interests. Even those things which cause us trouble and sorrow happen in harmony with his wisdom and love for us. Even the sting of sin and death fades when we see his grace and remember the perfect life and joy Jesus is coming to give us.

Remember God's grace and you will be "always thankful." Paul learned to see life from this point of view and so can we. Being thankful moves us to serve God and those around us. It reminds us that both joy and sorrow for a Christian are only different colors in the rainbow of God's love. And the best is yet to come!

Lord, fill my heart with thankfulness and my life with your love. Amen.

In keeping with God's promise we are looking forward to a new heaven and a new earth, the home of righteousness. (2 Peter 3:13)

A FEARLESS FUTURE

What will happen to us on judgment day? The Apostle Peter answered that very simply. "In keeping with God's promise we are looking forward to a new heaven and a new earth, the home of righteousness." On judgment day we will inherit a home of righteousness. That's good news. It is even better news when considered in contrast to what we have deserved.

When you woke up this morning, what was the first thing on your mind, "Today is Thursday; it's laundry day," or, "I only have an hour to get to work," or, "I wonder if it rained last night"? If you are like me, the morning's first efforts involve clearing the cobwebs from the brain and routinely mulling over the day's upcoming activities. Tomorrow morning let's try something different. Let's turn our attention to spiritual matters, "Where do I stand in relation to my God?"

If we take a look at ourselves in the mirror of God's perfect standards, the thought of standing before God isn't all that pleasant. He is holy; we are not. By the sin we are born with, by the wrong we do, and by the right we don't do, we deserve the worst. Our worries, doubts, greed, envy and anger have separated us from God's love. By all rights we have earned hell.

Thankfully, God is as merciful and forgiving as he is holy and just. He loaded onto his Son all our wrongs and transferred to us Jesus' perfection. Because of Jesus we won't get what we deserved; we will get what he earned. Now that is a truth worth holding onto as we begin each day. That is a truth worth holding onto every day, even to the end.

So what will happen to people on judgment day? When Christ Jesus appears in all his glory on that day, all the dead will be raised and brought before him with all the living. Those who have rejected God's mercy will be condemned, body and soul, to the eternal pain of hellfire and eternal separation from God's love. In the same moment, believers in Jesus will have their bodies glorified, and body and soul they will be with the Lord forever. As you sit on the edge of your bed tomorrow morning, ask yourself, "Where do I stand in relation to God? What will happen to me on judgment day?" Then think of the Savior, Jesus. He has prepared for us a home of righteousness. Therefore encourage each other with these words.

Abide, O faithful Savior,
Among us with your love;
Grant steadfastness and help us
To reach our home above. Amen.

If I am to go on living in the body, this will mean fruitful labor for me. Yet what shall I choose? I do not know! I am torn between the two: I desire to depart and be with Christ, which is better by far; but it is more necessary for you that I remain in the body. (Philippians 1:22-24)

COMMIT YOUR FUTURE INTO GOD'S HANDS

St. Paul was unsure of what kind of future he should wish for. What a blessing it would be if he would die and be with his Savior in heaven! On the other hand, what a joy it was to do the work of the Lord on this earth! Which should he choose? Which should he wish for?

Paul knew better than to try to make a decision on his own. He chose to leave the matter of his future in the Lord's hands. To do otherwise would be to play God. To decide for himself whether his life should continue or whether it should end would be playing God. Only the Giver of life also has the privilege of taking life.

We all know that millions of people today are trying to play God. Millions are trying to decide when life should come to an end. Thousands of suicides are committed yearly in our own land, many by teens and young adults. Millions of unborn children are being put to death by those who promote elective abortion. Some are also supporting euthanasia or "happy death," the ending of life prematurely to avoid the suffering and pain which may come with illness.

In every case individuals are playing God. They are taking from the Giver of life the privilege of determining when that life should come to an end. Our lifetime on this earth is so precious. It is the only opportunity we have to learn of our Savior's love. Dare we shorten that opportunity? The last few moments of life may be the ones in which a lost sinner finally learns of the Savior's love and forgiveness.

With St. Paul we commit our future into the loving hands of God. He knows what is best for us. If we have continued opportunity for fruitful labor in the Lord's vineyard, to God be the glory. If the God-appointed end of our life is drawing near and if we will soon be with our Savior in heaven, to God be the glory. What shall we hope for in the future? A difficult decision indeed. One we cannot make on our own. We commit our future into the hands of our loving and caring heavenly Father. He will make the correct decision for us. He will direct our life and our death for our eternal good.

Heavenly Father, into your loving hands I commit my future. May I serve you in love during my lifetime on this earth, and may I rejoice with you eternally in the next. In the Savior's name. Amen.

And we eagerly await a Savior from there, the Lord Jesus Christ, who, by the power that enables him to bring everything under his control, will transform our lowly bodies so that they will be like his glorious body. (Philippians 3:20, 21)

LOOK FORWARD TO CHRIST'S RETURN

We live now in a world that wallows in sin and is opposed to God's Word. And it is a constant vexation to us, as it was to righteous Lot while he lived in Sodom. But, like Sodom, our world and society will one day come to a crashing halt. And Christ, the great King and Judge, will appear. He will deal righteously with a sinful and rebellious mankind. And only those will escape who have washed their robes in the blood of the Lamb, that is, who believe in him as God's appointed sacrifice for their sins.

To us and all believers Jesus will appear, not as a fearful Judge, but as our Savior and glorious Lord. He will rescue us from this world; he will take us with him to that land which we have never seen but which is nonetheless our homeland.

And his will be a complete deliverance—not only from the evil influences of this world, but also from its evil effects. Each day we remain here we feel those effects: the quarreling and strife, the disappointments and frustrations, the worries and fears, the sickness and pain and weakness.

But when Jesus comes to deliver us, all that will be changed. The final episode in his plan of salvation will be to bring us out of this place into a marvelous place of joy, happiness and glory. Even our bodies will be changed for our new life there. Our present bodies corrupted by sin will be glorified at our resurrection, even as Jesus' body was at his resurrection. They will be cleansed from all weakness, from all sinful inclinations and from all death.

But for the present we are still on earth. And God has a reason for keeping us here for a while. It is our time of grace, during which God has graciously called us to a life of repentance and faith. It is also a time of opportunity—to bring that same gospel invitation to those still in darkness. But while we work and wait here, let us also turn our thoughts heavenward, to our homeland and to the one who will bring us there.

Our faithful God, through the gospel continue to assure us of our deliverance. Keep us faithful to our heavenly citizenship while here, that we may realize it there forever. Amen.

Therefore you do not lack any spiritual gift as you eagerly wait for our Lord Jesus Christ to be revealed. (1 Corinthians 1:7)

CALLED TO EXPECTANCY

When Mt. Vesuvius erupted, it completely destroyed the city of Pompeii. Many people were buried in the ruins under the hot lava and ashes. Many years later when excavations were begun, bodies were found in various places and postures. Some were found in the streets, as if they had been running to escape. Some were found in deep holes in the ground, as if they had gone there to hide. Where did they find the Roman sentinel? They found him standing at the city gate, where he had been placed by his captain, his hand still grasping his weapon. He had remained at his post—watchful and ready.

When the great day of judgment comes, will you and I be found watchful and ready?

God had made the Corinthians ready for that great day. By God's grace they did not lack any spiritual gift. God had done for them what he does for all Christians. He had graciously blessed them with everything they needed: the knowledge of their sin and its dreadful consequences; the good news of their complete pardon for Jesus' sake; and the needed information concerning judgment day, the resurrection from the dead and heaven.

The Christians in Corinth knew that they were completely forgiven. They knew that they had been declared righteous for Jesus' sake. They were certain that they had a home in heaven ready and waiting for them. With joyful anticipation and eagerness they could look to Jesus' coming.

So can you and I—and for the same reasons! "We wait for the blessed hope—the glorious appearing of our great God and Savior, Jesus Christ, who gave himself for us to redeem us." That day is going to be wonderful! It will be the first day of eternal bliss in heaven. Just imagine! We will be with Jesus in the special place he has prepared for us. It is all tremendously exciting. Like the Corinthians we also are filled with eager expectation as we "wait for our Lord Jesus Christ to be revealed."

The best way to spend our time until that day is, as Jesus put it, to be about our Father's business. That means using the talents and abilities God has entrusted to us for him and his kingdom. That means searching the Scriptures and continuing in prayer.

O blessed Redeemer, thank you for providing everything necessary to watch for your coming on judgment day. Fill me with joy and eager expectation as I wait for your return. Amen.

The Spirit himself testifies with our spirit that we are God's children. Now if we are children, then we are heirs—heirs of God and co-heirs with Christ, if indeed we share in his sufferings in order that we may also share in his glory. (Romans 8:16,17)

THE JOY OF HEAVEN

What a comfort it is for us to know that we are God's children through Christ's wonderful work of redemption! To this Paul adds for our eternal hope and joy, "Now if we are children, then we are heirs—heirs of God and co-heirs with Christ."

To what are we heirs? What is the inheritance of which Paul speaks? This inheritance is heaven which Jesus earned for us by his suffering, death and resurrection. And who of us is not interested in heaven? Who does not have a loved one in heaven? With the poet we say, "I'm but a stranger here; heaven is my home."

While the Bible does not tell us everything we might like to know about heaven, yet it does lift a corner of the veil to give us a glimpse of the glory that someday will be ours. In Psalm 16:11 we are told, "You will fill me with joy in your presence, with eternal pleasures at your right hand." St. Paul informs us in Philippians 3:21, ". . . the Lord Jesus will transform our lowly bodies so that they will be like his glorious body." St. Paul also gives us this picture: He [God] will wipe every tear from their eyes. There will be no more death or mourning or crying or pain, for the old order of things has passed away."

With our limited, human minds we are unable to picture fully the glory and beauty that some day will be ours. Nor do we have anything beautiful enough, or magnificent enough, or vast enough with which to compare it. Paul writes, "No eye has seen, no ear has heard, no mind has conceived what God has prepared for those who love him."

Furthermore, the joy and glories of heaven are eternal. In this world nothing remains. Great nations and kingdoms have arisen and fallen again. Even forests do not remain. They can be destroyed by fire or hewn down with an axe. But heaven and its joys are eternal.

The joy of heaven! This is the powerful and eternal message of the gospel. This is the message which pastors and teachers offer daily to their hearers.

Lord of Harvest, let there be
Joy and strength to work for Thee
Till the nations far and near
See Thy light and learn Thy fear. Amen.

And now, dear children, continue in him, so that when he appears we may be confident and unashamed before him at his coming. (1 John 2:28)

EAGERLY AWAIT CHRIST'S COMING

Jesus is coming. Are you ready? The thought of Jesus' second coming fills the unbeliever with terror. St. John saw a picture of that terror, and he recorded it for us in the book of Revelation. He wrote, "Then the kings of the earth, the princes the generals, the rich, the mighty and every slave and every free man hid in caves and among the rocks of the mountains. They called to the mountains and the rocks, 'Fall on us and hide us from the face of him who sits on the throne and from the wrath of the Lamb! For the great day of their wrath has come, and who can stand?' " (Revelation 6:15-17)

The unbeliever is right in fearing the coming judgment. What about us? Does the thought of judgment day make us uneasy? It does, because we are sinful human beings. We have violated God's will in thought, word and deed. We deserve nothing but God's wrath and punishment.

Yet, listen to the words of John in our text, "Continue in him, so that when he appears we may be confident and unashamed before him at his coming." We are God's children. Through faith in Jesus we possess the forgiveness of all our sins. The Lord has told us, "I, even I, am he who blots out your transgressions, for my own sake, and remembers your sins no more" (Isaiah 43:25).

When the Lord summons us to stand before him for judgment, our sins will not rise up to condemn us. Jesus paid for all of them by his death on the cross. We will not be ashamed to stand before God on that day, for we will be arrayed in the righteousness of our Savior.

It is no wonder that John tells us we may be confident and unashamed before Christ at his coming. Our confidence is not based on anything we have done. Our confidence is based on all that our God has done for us.

Jesus said, "I am coming soon" (Revelation 22:20). Are you ready? By the grace of God we are. We believe in Christ. We are God's children, clothed in Christ's righteousness. We pray, "Come, Lord Jesus."

**Jesus, Thy blood and righteousness
My beauty are, my glorious dress;
Midst flaming worlds, in these arrayed
With joy shall I lift up my head. Amen.**

56

We are confident, I say, and would prefer to be away from the body and at home with the Lord. (2 Corinthians 5:8)

FAITH PREFERS OUR HEAVENLY HOME

As seasons make their sweeping changes across the face of America, we often feel a stir of excitement within us. Feeling the warm summer sun, I can hardly wait to make my escape to a wonderful little vacation spot I've been dreaming about for a long, long time; a placid little glade nestled in the Adirondack Mountains of upstate New York. Perhaps you feel that way about a place where you long to be. I know St. Paul did.

Throughout the seasonal changes of his long and illustrious career, St. Paul longed to travel to the best vacation spot of all. St. Paul preferred his heavenly home. And by faith in Christ, he knew it had all been arranged. His flight was already booked.

The Apostle Paul was not suicidal. Nor did he despair of living because of the corruption of the world around him or because of his own sinfulness. Quite the contrary. St. Paul realized the importance of life as God's time of grace given to mankind to come to know Jesus as the Savior and escape God's wrath against sin. Being a messenger of God's grace, Paul wrote, "If I am to go on living in the body, this will mean fruitful labor for me."

Nonetheless, St. Paul did not regret that he would die. In fact, he looked forward to it. He longed to enter heaven and to enjoy to the full God's restored image of innocence, knowledge and righteousness. Like a little boy in a candy shop who wants to unwrap each piece, confident of its sweet taste, St. Paul wanted to shed his sinful nature in death, confident of Christ's forgiveness and the sweet taste of heaven which Jesus promised.

With the same confidence about Christ's forgiveness of our sins as St. Paul, based on the resurrection of our Savior, we too need not regret death or fear it. Even though death, the actual cessation of life in our bodies, is a mystery to us, we need not fear the outcome of death. Our departure has all been arranged by our loving God who sent his Son to die for us. By faith our flight has been logged into the Book of Life, taking us to an eternal vacation spot to be with our Lord Jesus Christ in our heavenly home.

Give me a faith full of divine confidence, dear Father, trusting in Christ's sacrifice for my sins, and opening heaven's door in death to an eternal paradise with my Savior. Amen.

When Christ, who is your life, appears, then you also will appear with him in glory. (Colossians 3:4)

TAKE THE HOPE THAT JESUS OFFERS

A young couple promised their four-year-old son that they would take him to the zoo. They did not set a specific time or date for the big event. Every day for the next week the little boy asked his parents if they would go to the zoo. Each time he was told, "Not today." Another week passed, then a month. As time went on the boy asked the question less frequently. He had almost given up all hope of going to the zoo when his father announced one sunny Saturday morning, "We are going to the zoo today." You can imagine the excitement of the little boy. His parents were finally making good on their promise.

The believers in the early Christian church waited anxiously for Jesus to return. They expected him to come in their lifetime. What joy filled the hearts of these people as they waited for the day Jesus would come! But Jesus did not come, in their time or the generations which followed. It was like the little boy and the promise that his parents made about going to the zoo. At first he was very excited about it, but when he did not see an immediate fulfillment, he began to place that promise in the background of his many other activities.

Now that almost two thousand years have elapsed since Jesus made his promise to return, our anticipation and excitement over his coming may have diminished. Therefore it's time to rekindle the comfort and joy in our hearts which his promise brings.

What a spectacular day that will be! Jesus will appear in all his glory to take his own to be with him in glory. Paul describes this event for us: "For the Lord himself will come down from heaven, with a loud command, with the voice of the archangel and with the trumpet call of God, and the dead in Christ will rise first. After that, we who are still alive and are left will be caught up with them in the clouds to meet the Lord in the air. And so we will be with the Lord forever. Therefore encourage each other with these words."

Are you suffering from illness or the loss of a loved one? Then take the hope that Christ offers and live. Depressed and worried about the economy and the future? Cling to Jesus' promise, and look forward to the eternal joy which he has won for you.

Savior, you have promised, "Because I live, you also will live." Make that promise a central theme in my life. Let me look forward to the day when this promise becomes a reality, and in the meantime help me to live a life of faith to your glory. Amen.

After that, we who are still alive and are left will be caught up with them in the clouds to meet the Lord in the air. (1 Thessalonians 4:17)

MEETING THE LORD IN THE AIR

Whenever some important dignitary arrives in our country, a grand welcoming party goes out to meet him. That will be the scene when our Lord comes on the clouds of heaven. The believers will meet their Lord in the air in welcome and join his triumphal descent. When that happens, they will be in the presence of the God who made them and redeemed them for himself.

Believers of the past longed to see their God face to face as he really is. Moses once made that request of God. But God told Moses, "You cannot see my face, for no one may see me and live." Believers of the present also long to see their Lord face to face, and they shall. For he has promised, "We shall see him as he is." But that will not become a reality until Jesus comes again and "will transform our lowly bodies so that they will be like his glorious body."

Right now our sinfulness prevents us from seeing God as he really is. But after the victorious Conqueror of death and hell appears on the clouds of heaven and his triumphant shout will have reached the dead in their graves and the believers will have come forth with their glorified bodies, the believers whom the Lord has left alive in the flesh at his coming will also experience his transforming power in their bodies. Then all the believers together will meet their Lord in his descent to punish his enemies and to grant his believers salvation in the new heavens and new earth.

Are we looking forward to that beautiful moment with eagerness and joyful anticipation when we shall be changed in the twinkling of an eye and meet the Lord in the air? Or do we lack enthusiasm to meet him because our conduct in word and action is not quite in keeping with the expectations of our coming Judge? Are we, as Adam and Eve were, afraid and more concerned about hiding than running to greet him with an enthusiastic welcome?

If our desire to meet him is somewhat less than fervent, let us remember just who it is we will meet. It is Jesus our righteous Judge through whom God has put away our sin and declared us fit to meet him. Yes, we are going to meet a Judge, but one who is loving, merciful and faithful. What a grand meeting we await!

Lord, let us look forward to meeting you with joy and faith. Amen.

God, who has called you into fellowship with his Son Jesus Christ our Lord, is faithful. (1 Corinthians 1:9)

GOD IS FAITHFUL

The movie ends and the credits glide by, a long list of all the people and activities involved in making the film. But in the story of our salvation there is only one credit, one name. All our hopes for this life and the next depend upon our Savior alone. He promises us, "I am trustworthy."

For this reason Paul always thanked God when he thought of the Christians at Corinth. Despite enemies outside and inside, the church would survive because God is faithful. His grace and reliability are the sure guarantee that all he has promised us will come to be.

Remember this simple truth: God is faithful! It comforts us because often we are not faithful to him. Our best intentions to trust and obey can crumble when we are threatened, unhappy or under pressure and temptation. Our love and patience with others may be shallow and weak. Even together as a church, we are sometimes slow to put into practice the very things we have united to say and do. The world we live in also makes it increasingly hard to follow Jesus and keep our consciences clear from sin.

If our hope of forgiveness and eternal life depended in any way upon us and our faithfulness, there simply would be no hope. But God is faithful! Through baptism and his message he has created new life in our hearts and minds. He called us into fellowship with his Son, making us members of his family, citizens of his kingdom of grace. God cares for us and leads us with his Word and Spirit as our Good Shepherd, our heavenly Father. The fellowship we have with God's Son and with all other believers in him is for our blessing and joy. Together we are ready and waiting for the coming of our Lord.

Just as the rainbow reminded Noah of God's faithfulness, God's Word will stand forever as proof that we can rely on him as our Savior. Do not take his promise lightly. God is also a faithful Judge, who will not be mocked by those who turn away. When Christ returns, he will be relentless in his judgment against those who do not believe. But by grace we are not among them. There is now no condemnation for those who are in Christ, who rely upon his work for our salvation. Our Savior is faithful.

When you are troubled by your sins and the evil of the world around you, take heart in this great promise: God is faithful!

Savior, thank you for your sure grace to us in Christ. Amen.

I can do everything through him who gives me strength. (Philippians 4:13)

COPING WITH LIFE—GOD'S WAY

Jesus once said, "If you have faith as small as a mustard seed, you can say to this mountain, 'Move from here to there' and it will move. Nothing will be impossible for you." Some people have mistakenly interpreted this verse and the above statement written by St. Paul to mean that if you set your mind to it, you can literally do anything. But God is not promising that we will be granted the magic power to do anything at all. He is speaking figuratively of the power of faith. Neither was Paul kidding himself into believing that he was omnipotent. But he was confident that through Christ he had the power to face whatever circumstances came along.

Some try to face life by being self-sufficient. They try to make contentment a human achievement. Paul's way—the Christian way—is to accept contentment as a divine gift and learn to be God-sufficient. Trusting in God's power rather than his own, Paul was able to face everything life could throw at him— hard work, imprisonment, floggings and beatings, threats of death and stonings, shipwreck, danger from all sides, lack of sleep, hunger, thirst, being cold and naked and the daily pressures of his concern for all the churches.

Without prayer and daily resting upon Christ's promises, St. Paul would not have been able to do it. Neither can we face the hardships of life without receiving the strength to endure from our God. We may not have the faith of a Paul or Luther, but even a weak faith is a true faith and a saving faith. And it becomes stronger with exercise.

With faith we can accomplish things that no unbeliever can ever hope to do. We can move God to grant our requests, providing they are in agreement with his will. As we bring the gospel to others we are instruments of the Holy Spirit, as he achieves the seemingly impossible conversion of unbelievers. In our own life we can overcome great obstacles. For whether we have little or much, at all times we have Jesus Christ. Walking with him and living in him we can be patient and hopeful in all things.

When my foolish heart asks why, quiet me with your words, "Be still, and know that I am God." Amen.

To keep me from becoming conceited because of these surpassingly great revelations, there was given me a thorn in my flesh, a messenger of Satan, to torment me. Three times I pleaded with the Lord to take it away from me. But he said to me, "My grace is sufficient for you, for my power is made perfect in weakness." Therefore I will boast all the more gladly about my weaknesses, so that Christ's power may rest on me. (2 Corinthians 12:7-9)

RELY ON THE LORD

This passage is quite often used together with that of Christ's prayer in Gethsemane to show that not all requests we bring to God in prayer are granted. Yet we must not lose sight of the truth that every Christian prayer is heard and answered by the Lord.

Paul asked the Lord for the removal of a nagging ailment, which he felt was impairing the spread of the Gospel. It seemed to Paul as if Satan were a boxer standing in his path and raining punches on his face. Paul could not make the progress he wanted to make.

Yet this "thorn in the flesh" served a good purpose in keeping Paul from becoming proud over the visions and revelations he had received. God simply could have told Paul that he had no right to question divine wisdom in this matter. But when Paul asked for relief, the Lord uncovered a truth that has become a well of encouragement for Christians ever since. God answered: "My grace is sufficient for you, for my power is made perfect in weakness." The ultimate purpose in all Christian suffering is that we may from experience develop a full, deep knowledge of our need to rely on the Lord and on his grace alone.

It is easy enough to say, "Oh, I depend on God for everything." But when all the props under us suddenly give way and we feel weak and helpless, then we learn from experience how much we really depend on God's grace alone in Christ.

We do not know what Paul's thorn in the flesh was. If he had wanted us to know, he would have told us. The fact that he simply calls it a "thorn in the flesh" makes it possible for us to compare it to our infirmities, whatever they may be. And the fact that he calls it a thorn "in the flesh" teaches us not to worry. God may permit the thorns to stick in our flesh for our good, but he will not let them touch our soul.

Dear Lord, help us to trust completely in your all-sufficient grace, realizing that it becomes most apparent in our weakness. Amen.

When he would not be dissuaded, we gave up and said, "The Lord's will be done." (Acts 21:14)

HIS WILL BE DONE

What Paul really needed from his friends was not their fretting and weeping, but encouragement. Instead of urging him to run from danger, they should have been strengthening him for the ordeal he faced. They could have reminded Paul that the Lord Jesus was directing his life and had promised to be with him always—no matter what.

Instead, it was Paul who strengthened them. The will of his Lord held no terrors for Paul. He knew Jesus loved him so much he had given his own life to rescue him from hell. Paul had experienced long years of Jesus' love and care for him. He, in turn, devoted all of his energies to telling people what Jesus had done to rescue all men from the certain disaster of hell. Paul was even ready to die for such a Lord.

When his friends saw they could not change Paul's mind, they fell silent and learned from his example of joyful acceptance to say, "The will of the Lord be done." After that, no more was said. No more needed to be said. Although at first they had been anxious about Paul's safety, they finally committed their hearts with confidence to their loving Lord. In faithful obedience, they submitted to his will. That settled it.

These Christians did not reluctantly give in to an unavoidable decree of God. They did not say with a fatalistic sigh, "Whatever will be, will be." They said, "The will of the Lord be done." Their acceptance of his will was not a surrender to fate, but an exercise of their faith. When they could not clearly see the good that God might do, they trusted that he still would do it. They believed, without knowing how, that whatever the Lord had decided should happen to Paul would be for the best. "In all things, God works for the good of those who love him" (Romans 8:28). Paul was not afraid of what might happen. And now, neither were his friends.

When we pray, "Thy will be done," we are to be ready to accept, as Paul did, whatever God may send our way. We too have seen God's faithful love for us, and we are sure that his will can bring nothing but good to us. Whether he sends pleasure or trials or even death, like Paul we should gladly accept it. It all comes from the same Lord. He is not punishing us. He only seeks our good.

His will be done!

**My God, my Father, make me strong,
When tasks of life seem hard and long,
To greet them with this triumph song:
Thy will be done. Amen.**

And we know that in all things God works for the good of those who love him, who have been called according to his purpose. (Romans 8:28)

GOD IS ON OUR SIDE

How can ill health, suffering, loss of possessions and other kinds of disaster possibly work together for good? Well, they don't work together for good for everyone. They only work for the good of those who love God. That makes the big difference.

The unbeliever simply cannot understand this. He can't understand how calamities in life can serve to draw one closer to God and to refine one's faith. He can't understand how afflictions, or what he would be inclined to call bad luck, can draw one away from the world and lead one to a richer prayer life and a stronger reliance on God. He can't possibly understand how trials and temptations uncover the evils in one's heart and at the same time make the faithfulness of a loving and gracious God stand out like the sun in a clear sky.

The child of God, on the other hand, understands all this very well. He has complete confidence in what his Savior tells him: "Are not two sparrows sold for a penny? Yet not one of them will fall to the ground apart from the will of your Father, and even the very hairs of your head are all numbered. So don't be afraid; you are worth more than many sparrows."

In view of this and with Christ's redeeming sacrifice as the perfect background, it would be strange indeed if we could not share Paul's complete confidence: "And we know that in all things God works for the good of those who love him." It is this confidence which not only makes life bearable for us but also provides us with a cheerful outlook. After all, God is on our side. Our hopes here and hereafter have a solid basis. Their fulfillment does not depend on our feeble, groping, spasmodic efforts. God himself has taken the matter in hand. We are secure no matter what. Listen to the Lord as he asks and answers the questions in the book of Joshua: "Have I not commanded you? Be strong and courageous. Do not be terrified; do not be discouraged, for the LORD your God will be with you wherever you go."

Ye fearful saints, fresh courage take;
The clouds ye so much dread
Are big with mercy and shall break
In blessings on your head.

Dear Lord, keep us secure even in affliction. Amen.

I have great sorrow and unceasing anguish in my heart. (Romans 9:2)

IN THE HOUR OF SORROW

Ever since the advent of sin, sorrow, disappointment, unceasing anguish and heartache have all been a part of life. Man has apparently realized this and has tried unsuccessfully to deal with the problem of sorrow and pain. The first way of dealing with sorrow is the way of the pleasure-seeker who says, "Avoid it." The second is the way of the stoic who says, "Grin and bear it." The third is the way of the person who says, "Deny it."

But there is a better way, and that is God's way. Through the Bible we come to the realization that nothing happens to us without God's permission. We must understand that despite sorrow and unceasing anguish we are still God's people through faith in Christ who gained for us complete pardon for our sins. We must remember that God reaches down from heaven and puts his everlasting arms beneath us to keep us from falling, to keep us on the way that leads past all our sorrow, pain and anguish into eternal life.

Sorrow is not a sign that God does not care for us, but rather it is a mark of his affection. The Bible states, "The Lord disciplines those he loves." We must realize that sometimes our sorrows will continue, and for this God may have a special purpose in mind. After all God did not remove all of the Apostle Paul's anguish. He proved that through this troubled man he could turn the world upside down. St. Paul was given the glorious chance to preach Christ crucified.

God does not always let us have our way. He leads us into his paths to make us into devout believers who rely solely on his grace. Our sorrow and anguish may be a time of testing, in which it becomes clear that we are sincere when we profess our complete dependence and trust in him.

It is easy to walk with God when he comforts and gladdens every step. But when he begins to discipline us and the road of life becomes a little bumpy, we might quickly discover that what we called faith was more satisfaction with our happy circumstances than trust in God. So one of the reasons God allows sorrow and anguish to come into our lives, is to strengthen and refine our faith. In the hour of sorrow we learn to rely on him more completely and cling to him more firmly.

Lord, I would clasp Thy hand in mine,
Nor ever murmur or repine:
Content, whatever lot I see,
Since 'tis my God that leadeth me. Amen.

For I am convinced that neither death nor life, neither angels nor demons, neither the present nor the future, nor any powers, neither height nor depth, nor anything else in all creation, will be able to separate us from the love of God that is in Christ Jesus our Lord. (Romans 8:38,39)

OUR ANCHOR IN THE STORMS OF LIFE

While at the shore of a lake on a stormy day, I noticed a sailboat anchored about a hundred yards offshore. The wind blew and the waves beat against that boat, threatening to dash it into pieces on the jagged rocks that lined the shore. But the sailboat, held tightly by the anchor and rope, survived the storm. Soon the storm was over.

As Christians, I am certain that there have been many times when we have felt very much like that sailboat. The storms of life can be pretty fierce. We seem like such a tiny craft in the midst of such a big and cruel lake. The wind and the waves beat against us, threatening to smash us to pieces.

At times like that it is good for us to remember the words of assurance which the Apostle Paul offers us in our text today. He reminds us of the fact that as long as God is with us, there is no power on earth and no power in hell that can ever tear us away from him. We have the strongest possible anchor. The storms will still come, but we have the assurance that God will help us

ride out those storms. Our boat will never sink, since God is with us always.

This is the same God who has promised us, "I give them eternal life, and they shall never perish; no one can snatch them out of my hand." The only way to get out of God's hand is if we jump out. No one, nothing can ever tear us away from God. Someone once compared life to a trip across the ocean on a slow-moving ship. We go from good weather to bad again and again. God pilots us through stormy seas until we finally reach the safe harbor of heaven where there will be no more storms to bother us.

No one is forcing God to do this, nor do we deserve his protection. He loves us so much that he wants to help us. If he loved us enough to send his Son to die for us, he certainly loves us enough to keep us safe from every earthly storm. Bonds of love tie us, anchor us to him — bonds which will never be broken.

In ev'ry high and stormy gale
My anchor holds within the veil.
On Christ, the solid Rock, I stand;
All other ground is sinking sand.

Lord, always keep us in your love. Amen.

In this you greatly rejoice, though now for a little while you may have had to suffer grief in all kinds of trials. These have come so that your faith—of greater worth than gold, which perishes even though refined by fire—may be proved genuine and may result in praise, glory and honor when Jesus Christ is revealed. (1 Peter 1:6,7)

ENCOURAGEMENT FOR EVERY TRIAL OF LIFE

Not long ago an American rock and roll star died. One of his fans said that she no longer had any reason to live. Idolaters lose everything when their idols perish. But it is not so with believers in Christ. We have become heirs of eternal life. In every trouble our faith "shines through the gloom and points us to the skies."

This portrait of Peter takes us far from the Sea of Galilee. He is a prisoner for the Lord in Rome not long before his execution under Nero. It is Peter's final exam in the school of faith. His faith in Jesus enables Peter to face death. The memory of Jesus' revelation at the Sea of Galilee enables Peter to encourage other believers. Peter holds out to them the hope that is ours in Christ's empty grave and beyond our grave: "an inheritance that can never perish, spoil or fade— kept in heaven for you"(1 Peter 1:4). Our faith may be tried in different ways. We may be in our own prison hospitalized with an incurable disease or awaiting the outcome of major surgery. Peter teaches us to see the divine purpose in every trial of faith. That hymn we sang in church on a Sunday may come to us in our present circumstance with fuller meaning and greater comfort:

The clouds ye so much dread
Are big with mercy and shall break
In blessings on your head.

(TLH 514:3)

Luther wrote, "If God disposes that you must suffer, accept it, console yourself with bliss that is eternal, not temporal. . . . Peter likens the gold that is tested by fire to the testing of faith by temptation and suffering. . . . Thus God imposes the cross on all Christians to purge them that faith may remain pure, as the Word is, so that one adheres to the Word alone and relies on nothing else. For we really need such purging every day because of the Old Adam."

May Peter's faith while a prisoner of the Lord show us the divine purpose in every trial of faith, that we, also, receive the end of our faith, the salvation of our souls!

Heavenly Father, may we learn from our Savior, as Peter did, that in every trial our faith is more precious than gold in your sight. Amen.

For when I am weak, then I am strong. (2 Corinthians 12:10)

STRENGTH IN WEAKNESS

Strength is an admirable quality. Everyone wants to be strong; no one wants to be weak. The physically strong always have an advantage over the physically weak. The world relies on such strength. Nations vie with each other for military might. They depend on the strength of arms to secure supremacy in the world and often use their strength to suppress the weak. Athletes train strenuously to develop strength, because the strong are the winners; the weak the losers.

What could Paul possibly mean when he says, "When I am weak, then I am strong"? How are these two opposites compatible? It is another of Paul's profound paradoxes. Just as he found joy in his sufferings, so he finds strength in his weakness. What an amazing display of God's grace!

It is the grace of God that makes us forget whatever human strength we may have and depend entirely upon the strength supplied by the Lord. The strong think they have no need of help and do not seek it. The weak know their need and lay hold of the Almighty's strength.

The accomplishments of the great heroes of faith were not the result of the human strengths these individuals possessed. Moses could only point to his weaknesses, the abilities he lacked when the Lord called upon him to lead his people out of Egypt. Never did Moses say, "I have led you out of slavery." It was always, "The Lord with his strength, with his mighty hand has brought us out of Egypt."

The gospel did not prevail because it originated in the great powers of the first century, in the learning of Greece and in the strength of Rome. It originated in the weakness of Palestine and Galilee. As Paul declared, "God chose the weak things of the world to shame the strong." The weakness of God is stronger than man's strength. In the weakness of his sufferings the strength of Christ was made perfect. His cross is the strength of Christianity.

The Lord manifests his strength in our weaknesses, too. The trials we endure, the sufferings we experience, the crosses we are called upon to bear display the grace of him who invites us, "Come to me, all you who are weary and burdened, and I will give you rest." May we cast all our anxiety upon him because he cares for us, and when we suffer according to his will, commit ourselves to our faithful Creator and continue to do good. Then in our weaknesses we are strong.

Strengthen my faith, O Lord, so that I may always see your grace in my afflictions and live in the strength that you supply. Amen.

But he said to me, "My grace is sufficient for you, for my power is made perfect in weakness." (2 Corinthians 12:9)

LOOK FOR GOD'S ANSWER

Often when we ask a question, we anticipate the answer. We already have in mind what the response to our question should be. But it happens very often, too, that the answer we receive isn't at all what we were looking for. Obviously, when we ask for something, we expect to receive what we are asking for. That's the reason we make the request, isn't it? So when we address our prayers to God and plead with him to help us in our need, we know how we want him to answer our prayer. We want him to remove the trouble that afflicts us. That's the answer we are looking for. Isn't that what it means to pray confidently, trusting in God's almighty power and in the assurance of his loving concern for our well-being? It certainly is. But remember, God answers our prayer according to his divine wisdom and not necessarily according to our wishes, no matter how frequently and fervently we plead with him to grant the answer we are looking for.

We can never say, then, that God isn't listening or that he doesn't care. His plans for us may just be different from what we think they should be. It is not for us to prescribe the time when he should help nor the manner in which he does. Sometimes we may be so determined that our way is the only way that we don't recognize God's answer when he gives it!

We certainly can learn from Paul's example. God did not give the answer Paul was looking for. But God did answer Paul's prayer—according to his own purpose and plan. "My grace is sufficient for you," he told Paul. He was reminding Paul that we are completely dependent on God's grace. By God's grace Paul was an apostle, and the effectiveness of his work as a chosen messenger of the gospel was not going to be diminished by his continuing to bear the thorn in his flesh. Paul's preaching of the Word would succeed because it is God who gives it success, and not because Paul was physically strong and healthy. God's power is all the more evident when he accomplishes his purpose in the weakness of the human instrument he has chosen to carry out his work.

Never forget that we are the objects of God's grace, just as Paul was. It is by his grace that we are his children and have the privilege of addressing him as our dear Father and placing our petitions before him. He will answer according to his grace and purpose.

We thank you, Lord, for every answer to our prayers. Amen.

And the God of all grace, who called you to his eternal glory in Christ, after you have suffered a little while, will himself restore you and make you strong, firm and steadfast. (1 Peter 5:10)

LOOK TO GOD FOR STRENGTH

As we look to the future, we must realize that our strength and our hope are entirely dependent on God's grace, the undeserved love he shows us. By grace God has sent his own Son to die for our sins. By grace God has called us into his kingdom. By grace through faith in Christ we can look forward to eternal glory.

We need to look to God for strength. That is Peter's God-inspired counsel to us. Without God we can accomplish nothing. It would be ridiculous for a mountain climber to try to scale a lofty peak without a rope or for an explorer to head down a river in a canoe without a paddle. Likewise it is foolish for anyone to think that he can face the rigors of life on his own without the strength and help God gives.

Peter directs us to the God of grace who will help us endure the sufferings of this life that will last for a short time when considered in the context of eternity. We can see the concern Peter has for the suffering Christians of his day who were sorely tested in their faith. But note how he again assures them that their sufferings are only for "a little while."

We need to have the proper attitude toward sufferings. We must realize that when we have to pass through God's refinery, it is his intent to purify the gold of our faith. Whatever draws us closer to God, however hard to bear at the moment, is a hidden blessing for which we should be eternally thankful. God had one Son without sin. He has no sons without suffering. It may be a cross for us now, but it will be a crown in the hereafter. We take heart from the words of the Apostle Paul, "And we know that in all things God works for the good of those who love him, who have been called according to his purpose."

God has promised to equip us with all that we need to endure suffering. He can restore us to oneness with him. He can keep us firm in true faith. He can make us steadfast in our allegiance to his Word. The God of all grace and power promises to guide us safely through to eternal glory. What a blessed assurance that is!

Rock of ages, cleft for me,
Let me hide myself in thee.

God of grace, make us strong, firm and steadfast in Christ. Amen.

To the praise of his glorious grace, which he has freely given us in the One he loves. (Ephesians 1:6)

AMAZING GRACE

What is grace? To some it is the name of a pretty girl they know. To others grace is what you say before you eat. To still others grace is good manners, or the action of a performer in a ballet. To the sinner, grace is the unmerited mercy of an all-loving God.

Grace is an amazing thing. It is hard to define. It is love, but more than love. It is undeserved love. This grace has been freely given to us by God.

God's grace flows freely, daily, bountifully. It is not a slow drip, drip, drip from the faucet of his love. It is grace sufficient to cover all our sins, no matter how bad they are or how often they have been repeated. It is grace in abundance for every day of our lives. It greets us in the morning, fills our days with the sunshine of God's love, and covers us warmly through the night.

God's grace flows freely in another sense. It is ours without price. A good thing, for we could never begin to pay for our forgiveness. The national debt exceeds billions of dollars. Even if we laid all of this money at the feet of the Almighty, it would not be sufficient to purchase forgiveness for a single sin. But what we could not earn or buy, God gives to us freely "in the One he loves."

Not that this grace is cheap. It has been paid for by the tremendous price of the suffering and death of the holy Son of God, the "One he loves." Twice God declared his love for his Son. At Jesus' baptism God called from heaven in a loud voice, "This is my Son, whom I love." On the Mount of Transfiguration the disciples heard the voice from the cloud proclaim, "This is my Son, whom I love." God's grace flows freely in his beloved Son, Jesus Christ.

It is this Savior whose perfect life, mighty death in payment for sins and victorious resurrection on the third day purchased our forgiveness. Thus God provided a fountain of forgiveness and mercy for all people of all generations. This free-flowing grace of God deserves our praises now and throughout eternity.

Lord God, heavenly Father, we praise you for the glorious grace that purchased our eternal forgiveness. We confess that what we could not pay for or earn has been freely given us in our Savior, the One you love, and the One we love. Amen.

Who has known the mind of the Lord? (Romans 11:34)

KNOWING THE MIND OF THE LORD

What an amazing creation of God is the human mind! However, most attention these days is given to computers. How much information can the computer store? How fast can it operate? We often tend to forget that each of us has a mind which puts even the most powerful computers to shame.

It has been said we use only a small portion of our brains. Even at that our minds are capable of some astounding things. Consider the speed of the brain in eye-hand coordination. The eye sees a ball speeding our way and in an instant sends a message to the brain which in turn sends a message to the hand to reach up to catch it. We think a home computer is more than adequate if it has a memory capacity of 128K, but just consider the memory capacity of the human brain. It has been said that everything we have ever known or experienced is in our minds somewhere. Consider the human mind's ability to reason and to make decisions. Show me a computer which can do these things as well, or do them at all for that matter. Even though more is being learned about the human mind all the time, we still don't understand its many-faceted complexities, intricacies and abilities.

How then can we expect to understand the mind of the Lord? How can we ever hope to investigate the mind of him who knows absolutely everything? How can we whose minds are corrupted by sin expect to comprehend the mind of the holy and righteous God? Isn't that completely presumptuous? Yes, for man by nature it is.

"But we have the mind of Christ," Paul says in 1 Corinthians 2:16. That means that by God's Word the Spirit reveals the mind of the Lord to us. As believers we know that God thinks thoughts of love and kindness toward us in Christ Jesus. We learn that because of Christ's death on the cross there is no longer in God's mind any wrath or hatred toward us. We understand that God has only our best interests in mind, that he wants only what is best for us in our lives now, and that he wants us with him in heaven forever. In God's Word we come to know the mind of the Lord in another sense. We understand the way God wants us to think and speak and live.

"Who has known the mind of the Lord?" No computer ever built will be able to know God's mind. The greatest minds of men have never nor will they ever discover the mind of the Lord by their own powers. Only believers know the mind of God because he has revealed it to them in his Word.

Lord, help me to know your mind ever better through the daily study of your Word. Amen.

We have not received the spirit of the world but the Spirit who is from God, that we may understand what God has freely given us. (1 Corinthians 2:12)

COUNTLESS BLESSINGS OF FAITH

By means of human reasoning we cannot bring ourselves into the Christian faith, just as we cannot use worldly wisdom to argue anyone else into believing. Dr. Martin Luther understood this well when he wrote in his Small Catechism, "I cannot by my own thinking or choosing believe in Jesus Christ, my Lord, or come to Him."

By nature we have neither the strength nor wisdom to believe. For we are spiritually dead. And a spiritually dead person can no more enable himself to believe in Jesus, than a physically dead person can make himself alive again. He needs someone outside himself to do that for him. God has done it for us.

This is why the Apostle Paul declared that he spoke not by the spirit of the world but rather by God's Spirit. Through the Holy Ghost Paul knew God's wonderful wisdom. This is also the only way anyone will ever know that wisdom.

The Holy Spirit comes to us as infants through God's Word and Holy Baptism, "the washing of regeneration and renewing of the Holy Ghost." Older ones hear God's Word, and by his grace the Holy Spirit works faith in Christ in their hearts. Paul tells us that "no man can say that Jesus is the Lord, but by the Holy Ghost." He also says that faith in Christ is a gift of God: "For it is by grace you have been saved, through faith—and this is not from yourselves, it is the gift of God—not by works, so that no one can boast."

The Holy Spirit revealed many blessings to us when he brought us to faith in Jesus Christ. We now trust in Jesus as our Savior. We know our sins are fully and completely forgiven for Jesus' sake. We are at peace with God. We can pray to our dear heavenly Father "as dear children ask their dear father." We know that when we die our soul will be with the Lord in heaven. We know that our body will be resurrected a glorious body and reunited with our souls on the Last Day. We know we will spend eternity in our Father's magnificent mansions above in heaven. This is God's glorious promise to us through Jesus Christ our Lord.

These are some of the countless blessings that come with a Spirit-worked faith. Surely God has been gracious to us! May our hearts be filled with thankfulness—now and forever.

**Into Christ baptized,
Grant that we may be
Day and night, dear Spirit,
Perfected by Thee. Amen.**

As the Scripture says, "Anyone who trusts in him will never be put to shame." For there is no difference between Jew and Gentile—the same Lord is Lord of all and richly blesses all who call on him. (Romans 10:11,12)

NO MATTER WHO YOU ARE!

Whose Son is he? The people who know the answer to this question are a most privileged people!

This wonderful privilege, though, is not reserved for a select few. This wonderful privilege is freely offered to all. God will have all people to come to know the truths about his Son, Jesus Christ.

God is no respecter of persons. He does not practice discrimination on the basis of age, sex, race, or social status. He knows that there is no difference. He knows that all have sinned. He knows that all need a Savior. There are no exceptions. Both Cain and Abel needed a Savior. Both Pharaoh and Moses needed a Savior. Both Saul and David needed a Savior. Both Mary Magdalene and Mary, the mother of Jesus, needed a Savior. Both John and Judas needed a Savior. Both the prodigal son and his elder brother needed a Savior. Both you and I need a Savior. The need is universal, and God met that need.

The Bible reveals that God loved the world . . . that he gave his only-begotten Son for the world . . . and that he invites the world to come to know and believe in his Son. Thus, "the Scripture says, 'Whosoever believeth on him shall not be ashamed.'"(KJV) The word "whosoever" is all-inclusive. Richard Baxter, a noted preacher in Scotland, claimed that he could not thank God enough for the word "whosoever." It meant more to him, he said, than if the Holy Spirit had put his own name into the Bible. He declared, "If God had said that there was mercy for Richard Baxter, I would have thought that he must have meant another Richard Baxter. However, when he says 'whosoever,' I know that he means me!"

Not one of us is outside the circle of God's love. The love of God is not exclusive. It is all-inclusive. Whosoever we are, we are invited to learn the saving truths about Jesus Christ. However, what we know of Jesus Christ literally must be taken to heart. It is possible, you see, to miss God's promise of forgiveness and life by sixteen inches. That, by the way, is the distance between the head and the heart. It is not enough to know Jesus intellectually with our minds. We must also know him intimately with our hearts.

Lord, whosoever we are, may we always embrace you with all of our mind and heart. Amen.

Those he (God) called, he also justified. (Romans 8:30)

GOD'S GRACE COMES TO OUR RESCUE

A frightened man enters the courtroom and nervously faces the judge and jury. He is charged with first degree murder. The death penalty is his sentence, should he be found guilty. The physical evidence seems to be irrefutable. Yet he pleads not guilty.

The accused man is hoping that his lawyer can suppress the damaging evidence. Maybe the investigating officer made a technical mistake in searching the scene of the crime. Maybe the arresting officer failed in properly reading him his rights. Maybe some of the jurors can be swayed with emotional appeals so that the verdict will be guilty of manslaughter or even a lesser crime. Maybe, just maybe, he can get out of the charge completely. But it may take months or years as the case works its way through appeal after appeal. How agonizing this process is for the accused, not to mention the continuing burden of guilt on his conscience.

Then what is it going to be like to stand before the judgment seat of God? The evidence is absolutely irrefutable. We are sinners many times over. No earthly testimony or human argumentation can lessen the guilt. Justice demands the eternal death penalty. That means never-ending suffering in the fires of hell. The situation is hopeless.

Such is our rightful condition before the eternal tribunal of the Lord. But once again in his grace our God comes to the rescue. With the absolute judicial power he possesses, he simply declares us not guilty. He announces that all convicting evidence has been removed and that all charges have been dropped. He proclaims that we are justified, that is, righteous in his sight.

How can God do this and still be a holy and just God? Simple. With love for us sinners he planned for our justification by sending his Son to be our Redeemer. The blood of Jesus blots out the mountains of evidence against us. Not only has Jesus sacrificed himself for us, but he also pleads our case before the Father. For his sake our sins are forgiven. "All . . . are justified freely by his grace through the redemption that came by Christ Jesus" (Romans 3:24). And we don't have to wait in agony for the verdict. We are justified here and now. Once again our Lord has done it all.

O Lord, it is because of your amazing grace alone that you forgive a sinner such as me. Help me to serve you with my life, for Jesus' sake. Amen.

Oh, the depth of the riches of the wisdom and knowledge of God! (Romans 11:33)

PLUMBING THE DEPTHS OF GOD'S GRACE

Most of man's knowledge about the sea bottom has been gained over the years by the use of special instruments. For many years the depth of water was measured with a sounding lead. A ball of lead was attached to a wire rope. The lead was dropped into the ocean, and the rope was let out until the lead touched the bottom. The rope went over a wheel which measured the length of rope paid out. Sometimes it took several hours to make one sounding in deep water.

In recent years a new method called sonic sounding has been developed. Some waves sent down from the ship are reflected from the bottom, so that an accurate measurement of the depth becomes possible. In this way it has been learned, for example, that the Pacific Ocean off Mindanao is over six and a half miles deep!

How does one plumb the depths of God? Is there a wire long enough to measure the greatness of God? Can we somehow measure reflected sound waves to learn about God? How does one begin to fathom the knowledge of One who knows absolutely everything there is to know? How does one measure infinite wisdom? Can the creature plumb the depths of the Creator? The fact is that if all the greatest minds in the history of the world were to use their combined intelligence and learning they still could not even begin to plumb the depths of God's wisdom.

That does not mean that we are totally ignorant of God's wisdom and knowledge. The works of God all around us—the universe, the earth, the creatures, our own bodies—lead us to join the psalmist in saying, "In wisdom you made them all" (Psalm 104:24).

Paul certainly was aware of the greatness of the wisdom of God revealed in the creation. But in our text Paul sings a song praising the greatness of God's wisdom revealed to us in the gospel of Christ. From eternity God determined to send his Son into the world to die on the cross for the sins of all mankind. No human being ever conceived such a wise plan. In fact, to the mind of sinful man it seems like nothing but foolishness. Only to the one in whom the Spirit has worked is it true wisdom. "Oh, the depth of the riches of the wisdom and knowledge of God!" Let us join Paul in falling on our knees in worshiping the God of our salvation.

Lord, help me always to realize that knowing you as my Savior is true wisdom. Amen.

For from him and through him and to him are all things. (Romans 11:36)

GOD'S BLANK CHECK

Charles Steinmetz, the great electrical engineer and inventor, never received a fixed salary from those who sponsored him. From time to time his backers would give him a book of blank checks. Whatever he needed, great or small, he only had to fill in the amount on a check, sign his name and present it to the bank.

Not too bad an arrangement! It surely would help at bill-paying time if one never had to worry about the checkbook balance.

Steinmetz's backers could eventually have run out of money, however. Surely Steinmetz's friends were helpless in keeping him from getting sick. They couldn't give him the strength, knowledge and ability he needed to do his work.

We have an infinitely better arrangement with God. God provides for the needs of all people. God is the origin of all things. From his creating hand came the universe, the earth and all creatures. From him comes all we need for our bodies and lives. Rain, sunshine, crops, food, drink and shelter all come from God. If God were to withdraw his sustaining hand for even an instant we would have nothing and we could not live.

Through him you and I and all creatures continue to exist. "In him we live and move and have our being" (Acts 17:28). We couldn't take a breath; our hearts couldn't beat; we couldn't put one foot in front of another if it weren't for God. He is not only present in our world but in our very beings.

From him alone also comes our salvation. It is all the work of his grace in Christ Jesus. Through him alone come all our spiritual blessings.

In a sense God has given us a blank check. It is made out to us, and it is signed in Jesus' blood. We can fill in the amount. Do we desire a stronger faith? We can write it in, and he will give it. Do we wish to see more fruits of faith in our lives? They are ours. Are there things we need for our bodies and lives? We can fill them in, and he will give them to us as he knows best. "From him and through him are all things."

Also "to him are all things." He is the final goal of the universe and all created things. All have been created to give praise and glory to his name.

Lord, help me remember that everything I am and everything I need comes from you. Help me praise you with my whole being. Amen.

For in him you have been enriched in every way—in all your speaking and in all your knowledge. (1 Corinthians 1:5)

THE BEST LIFE HAS TO OFFER

Grandpa reached into his pocket and brought out two coins for Lois and her little sister. Lois and Grandpa smiled at each other; this was their special joke. Grandpa held up the coins for the youngest to see and asked her, "Now, which one would you like, this big nickel or this little dime?" She quickly took the nickel, and Grandpa laughed as he gave Lois the dime. Little sister always took the nickel!

Our idea of what is best, of what offers us the greatest worth, is not always so good. Someone who knows better must teach us the true value of things. We need to learn where and how to find life's treasures.

Paul thanked God for teaching these things to the Christians at Corinth and for blessing them. They had become rich in every way. How? Paul says, "*In him* you have been enriched," that is, in Jesus. Even unbelievers benefit from God's creation, the physical wealth of this world. But only in Jesus Christ can a person become rich, rich in every way—physically, spiritually and eternally.

In Christ, we not only have all we need for our bodies and life, but also rich spiritual gifts. Love, joy, peace and hope are all ours through his Holy Spirit. We also have the precious promise that Jesus is coming again. We will be free forever from sin, death and sadness. The priceless treasure of an eternal inheritance with the Lord is ours already, set aside for us until Jesus returns.

The grace of God had enriched the Corinthians with a clear understanding of these riches in Christ. They had received both the desire and the skill to share the good news about their Savior with others. Joy in a new life with Christ, a change of heart about sin, an eager anticipation of Christ's return—all these blessings shone forth in their thinking and speaking. They were rich. Even the problems of this church could not dim the gleam of the treasures the believers shared.

Where do you look for the best life has to offer? Money, a fine house and expensive entertainment are wonderful things, yet they often disappoint us. And it's no secret that these things do not last. The prophet Isaiah gave us this map to better riches: "[The Lord] will be the sure foundation for your times, a rich store of salvation, wisdom and knowledge; the fear of the Lord is the key to this treasure." Look to the Savior for the best life has to offer. In him, we are rich in every way.

Lord, give us also the best riches life offers. Amen.

Grace and peace to you from God our Father and the Lord Jesus Christ. (1 Corinthians 1:3)

GRACE AND PEACE IN CHRIST

Each star in the night sky has a wonderful secret. What we see as only a twinkle of light is actually the blaze of a brilliant, distant sun. Consider what that tiny sparkle really is, and you will appreciate a star's true majesty and power.

Our Bible verse is just a brief thought. But it's like a star. Although this verse is small, it has a wonderful message. Consider what these words are saying, and you will appreciate the true majesty and power of our Savior's love for us.

The Gentiles once greeted one another with a Greek word that resembled "grace." The Jews said and still say, "Shalom," meaning "Peace." The Holy Spirit guided Paul to join these two thoughts as a special greeting in his New Testament letters. For Christians of all time, these words are like a diamond ring on a bride's finger. They remind us of love and faithfulness, the Father's love-in-action for us in Christ.

Grace points to the way God feels about us and treats us. Grace is kindness, generosity and love shown even to those who do not deserve them. Because we are all sinners, we deserved punishment. But God gives us love. We often forget to thank him. We often live as though he isn't even there and as though he will never return. But the Lord cares for us. He has forgiven our sins through Jesus. He watches over us and blesses us. God shows us grace.

Grace brings us peace with God. This peace does not come from us. It isn't just how we feel or something we must make for God. Jesus created this peace for us. He did this by keeping his Father's law perfectly for us and by suffering on the cross the punishment for our sins. The Holy Spirit reminds us of what Jesus has done. Through God's Word, the peace we have moves us to trust the Lord more and more. It moves us to live thankful lives in harmony with God's Word.

Trouble, worry and our own sinful weakness often bring a shadow over this peace. But they can never overcome it. How can we be sure? God our Father and his Son our Lord have created grace and peace for us. The cross guarantees this gift forever. We are thus ready and waiting for Christ's return.

What a wonderful message is in this one little verse! Whenever you hear these words, remember God's great gift of love to you!

Lord, may my life be a thankful answer to your grace and peace. Amen.

And he gave orders to stop the chariot. Then both Philip and the eunuch went down into the water and Philip baptized him. When they came up out of the water, the Spirit of the Lord suddenly took Philip away, and the eunuch did not see him again, but went on his way rejoicing. (Acts 8:38,39)

GOD'S GRACE IN BAPTISM

After it was all over, it must have seemed like a dream to the Ethiopian. What kind of man was this, who came to him, explained God's word to him, baptized him and then vanished! But the Ethiopian knew it was real. He now knew that Jesus Christ was the Lamb in Isaiah's prophecy, his Savior; he had been baptized; he really had an answer to the questions of his heart. And he was glad. As he continued his journey, he continued to rejoice.

This is perhaps one of the most unusual baptisms in history, but it is basically no different from yours and mine. Every Christian baptism is the same. It is a means by which God gives us the forgiveness of sins. No wonder the Ethiopian was happy! Through his baptism he was firmly established in his newly-received faith in Jesus. He was beginning to discover what many other Christians have experienced through their baptisms.

Baptism means life! Life with God. By baptism we have been born again so that we can live in God . . . live by God . . . live for God. Baptism has broken the chains of sin, death and hell. Baptism has set us free in Christ; and it gives us boldness to go into battle against temptation. Baptism delivers the victory of Jesus' death and resurrection to us. As St. Paul says in his letter to the Romans (6:4): "We were therefore buried with him through baptism into death in order that, just as Christ was raised from the dead through the glory of the Father, we too may live a new life."

Is it any surprise that the Ethiopian went on his way home rejoicing? That is the same joy we have available to us in our baptism. In our baptism we find new power to love and to live with God. In baptism God has lavished on us the joy of forgiveness and has given us a panoramic view of heaven. No matter how many years have passed since you were baptized, your baptism is still and will always be valid. It is a solid rock and source of spiritual refreshment and renewal. In a world burdened with many and daily troubles, in a life beset by many and powerful temptations, that is good news—the very Good News of the gospel of Christ.

O Lord, how good and faithful you are in spite of my sinfulness and unfaithfulness. As your baptized child, I return to you for forgiveness and for a renewed zeal to do your will; in Jesus' name. Amen.

Who though faith are shielded by God's power until the coming of the salvation that is ready to be revealed in the last time. (1 Peter 1:5)

THANK GOD YOU'RE SAFE

Yes, it's great to be alive—spiritually alive in Christ, filled with a living hope as heirs of God. Yet being a Christian in this world is not a "piece of cake." In fact, without the grace of God it would be impossible to remain a Christian.

The fact that we are alive, born again children of God, means that our life will be a struggle, a daily battle. The unholy three, the devil, the sinful world and our sinful flesh, gang up on us. They work hard to weaken and destroy our faith and our spiritual life.

"Our struggle," Paul wrote, "is not against flesh and blood, but against the rulers, against the authorities, against the powers of this dark world and against the spiritual forces of evil in the heavenly realms." Indeed, the devil's schemes can sometimes make us wonder whether it is so great to be alive. The fierce temptations we face, the sins we struggle against make us wonder, "How can I ever win? How can I hope to remain a believing child of God against such odds?"

One thing is sure—if it came down to us against Satan, if it were only up to us and our own strength and will, the battle would be lost. Peter, for one, discovered that we cannot rely on our own powers.

But Peter himself here encourages us to know and to trust that we are safe. The unholy three—devil, world and flesh—cannot win the battle and steal our salvation from us. "Through faith you are shielded by God's power," Peter tells us, from the present moment until the time when Jesus comes again to give us our inheritance of eternal glory.

Thank God for his mercy! It really is great to be alive in Christ, to know that our gracious God will not allow us to fall back into the hands of Satan and into spiritual and eternal death. He will shield us, guard and keep us till the last day.

But let's be sure that we don't miss two important words, "through faith." God's promise does not give us the right to fall asleep and to neglect our faith and spiritual life. God keeps us in faith by his Spirit through the preaching of the gospel and the sacrament of the altar. As we faithfully use them, he keeps us; we will be safe.

Heavenly Father, guard and keep us so that the unholy three may not deceive us or lead us into false belief, despair and other great and shameful sins; and though we are tempted by them, enable us to overcome and win the victory, through our Lord Jesus Christ. Amen.

In this way, love is made complete among us so that we will have confidence on the day of judgment, because in this world we are like him. (1 John 4:17)

BUILD YOUR PRESENT ON THE FUTURE

An evangelism approach used by some congregations opens with the question, "If you were to die tonight, do you know for certain where you'd be?" People who look at themselves and their lives for the answer don't know for sure—and are afraid of the question. People who look to God's love in the death and resurrection of Jesus Christ know certainly that their death will mark the beginning of eternal life with their Lord. God's love in Christ offers us that wonderful assurance. And in love God proposed that we might be able to approach the great day of judgment boldly.

But isn't it very cocky and presumptuous to say we know that our eternal destiny with Jesus is sure? No! To say anything less would be a doubting denial of what Jesus accomplished on the cross. St. John says that we have been made like Jesus, even though we are still in the world. That is not to say we have reached perfection here, but that we are now the adopted sons and daughters of God. We are the objects of our Father's love, as Christ was loved by his Father. We have been credited with the perfectly righteous life Jesus lived for us. He has paid for and removed our sins, which would otherwise have banished us forever from God's presence. So even though we are still on this side of judgment day, we who in baptism have "put on Christ" (Galatians 3:27) face that day with boldness.

But how is it that we should be bold? Doesn't the Bible tell us to be meek and humble? It tells us to be all of these at once: meek and humble as we evaluate ourselves and our miserable works, which are all tainted by sin; but bold and confident as we see the grand and glorious works of Christ and his righteousness, all of which belong to us by faith.

Our Christian hope is not some vague wish for the future. It is the eager anticipation of an assured future that fills our present with meaning. We are not to build our future upon the present, but our present upon the future. The empty cross points to our crown of glory in heaven. It gives us new courage. It lifts up our drooping spirits. And it brightens up our gloomy faces with the sure message that Christ is our Savior, God is our Father, and heaven is our home.

Fix our eyes on the crown of eternal glory your love has secured for us, dear Savior, that we may live boldly for you in our time of grace. Amen.

In this you greatly rejoice, though now for a little while you may have had to suffer grief in all kinds of trials. (1 Peter 1:6)

HOPE OUTLASTS TROUBLE

There was a time when the prophet Elijah was so overwhelmed by the difficulties of his work that he simply gave up and prayed to die. It is a feeling many since Elijah's day have shared. Life is indeed difficult. At times it may seem unbearable. For many, suicide seems the only answer, the easy way out.

"To end it all. To be rid of my suffering. To put my treatments behind me." How simple it all seems.

A man once said, "When you say a situation or a person is hopeless, you are slamming the door in the face of God." Yes, it's not easy to lie in a hospital bed day after day. Nor is it fun to come home when somebody in the family believes the only answer to life comes out of a bottle. But even these problems are not too big for God. If you give up on them, if you give up on life, you are really giving up on God.

How can you give up on God when he brought you into life? How can you give up on God when he gave his one and only Son to be your Savior? How can you give up on God when he has been with you with his word on the pages of the Bible?

Do not give up on him who has promised, "Never will I leave you; never will I forsake you." God will not give up on you.

We simply need to remember that every problem in life is only temporary. We can outlast it. God may well bring our difficulties to a close with the new dawn. In this we can greatly rejoice.

But what of the person who has been told his illness is terminal? How can we call that temporary? If we will just look to the garden where a man by the name of Joseph of Arimathea owned a burial site, we will note that the grave previously occupied now stands empty. Christ has conquered death. And we now have the hope of life in heaven. In Christ we can outlast any problem, even death.

When Elijah prayed that God would let him die, God instead patiently listened to his troubles and then renewed his hope in the promises of the Lord. God is listening to you. Talk to him in prayer. Listen to him through his Word. And then conquer each day with hope in a God who truly cares for you.

O my Savior, help me to endure my griefs and to sing your praises. Amen.

So that through endurance and the encouragement of the Scriptures we might have hope. (Romans 15:4)

THERE'S ALWAYS HOPE FOR TOMORROW

"The sun'll come out tomorrow," Little Orphan Annie sang in the movie. Anytime she got depressed and began to feel hopeless, she'd sing that song. Suddenly she felt better; she had hope for a brighter future. She also sang this song for others. And no matter how depressed they were, she got them to have hope for tomorrow.

All of us want to have hope. Sometimes little gimmicks help to get us out of the dumps. There's an ice cream cone for a little leaguer who struck out four times in the game. How about a kiss for a little girl who scraped her knee rollerskating? Mother who has had the worst day of her life gets taken out for dinner.

But even the best gimmick will let us down. The hurt may be just too painful for a kiss to take it away. The tragedy may be just too devastating for an ice cream cone or even dinner out to make us feel better. Things can get so bad sometimes that there doesn't seem to be any hope, and no cute song from an adorable little girl will make us feel better. But even then, there is hope.

In the Scriptures we learn that there's always hope for tomorrow.

These were written "so that through endurance and the encouragement of the Scriptures we might have hope." Endurance is the ability to stand up under heavy pressure and hold on, like a weight lifter who raises a barbell and holds it over his head. Endurance is our ability to put up with difficulties and come through. And this endurance in faith and life comes from the Bible.

As we read the Bible, God talks to us. He encourages us. He gives us the strength to endure. He gives us examples of how he has delivered his people in the past. He says, "I still have the same power and the same love to help you today."

When things look hopeless, look to the Bible, and find hope. Do you need help? God can provide it. Do you need forgiveness? God will give it. Do you need peace of mind? God has promised it and will give it to you. When things look hopeless, turn to the Scriptures, which give you encouragement and endurance. For with the Word of God, there's always hope for tomorrow.

Holy Spirit, turn me to your Word and fill me with the endurance and encouragement that only your Word can give. In this way give me hope for all my tomorrows. Amen.

The creation waits in eager expectation for the sons of God to be revealed. (Romans 8:19)

A WORD ABOUT THE FUTURE

The young and the young at heart often find it difficult to wait. It might be a party, a reunion with a friend, or some other big event that they are looking forward to. Anticipation fills their whole being. They just can't wait until the big day comes. If you have ever experienced that kind of anticipation, then you will certainly be able to understand our word about life for today.

In this verse we are told that the creation is on pins and needles as it waits for the completion of God's promises to his people. The creation waits with anticipation for the formation of the new heavens and earth, for the day when the resurrected and glorified saints will stand face to face with their God in glory. What a great day that will be!

Some people live their lives fearing their past, others are filled with doubts about the present and many are totally uncertain about the future. A few have hope that the future will be better but have no valid grounds on which to base that hope.

To live in fear, to live in doubt or to live with a groundless hope are not necessary evils in life. Jesus Christ calms fear, cancels doubt and supplies firm ground for a certain hope. Fear is calmed because, thanks to Jesus, all is right between sinful mortals and God. Doubt is canceled because, "If God is for us, who can be against us?" Hope is firmly established since Jesus declared, "Because I live, you also will live."

By God's grace we can look forward to each succeeding day. We can look forward with hope, peace and joy. Life is not a joke—with us as its target. In Christ, life is a wonderful blessing to be lived in the sure hope of ever better things to come.

Each day brings us closer to glory. With each passing day, the anticipation builds also in the creature world as the time for the revealing of God's sons draws near. "Dear friends, now we are children of God, and what we will be has not yet been made known. But we know that when he appears, we shall be like him, for we shall see him as he is."

"Forever with the Lord!"
O Father, 'tis Thy will.
The promise of that faithful word
E'en here to me fulfill. Amen.

In his great mercy he (God) has given us new birth into a living hope through the resurrection of Jesus Christ from the dead. (1 Peter 1:3)

THE CHRISTIAN'S LIVING HOPE

A very important part of every person's life is hope. There is scarcely a day when we do not indicate in some way or another that we are hoping for something. "I hope that package comes in today's mail." "I hope the dentist does not find any cavities in my teeth." "I hope we have meat loaf for dinner."

Very often this word "hope" expresses nothing more than a fond wish. Even though the sky may be overcast with dark, threatening clouds, you may say, "I hope it doesn't rain today." You may say that even though you are reconciled to the fact that rain is almost inevitable.

The Bible uses this word "hope" in a different way. It uses it in the sense of a sure hope or a certain hope. When we speak about our hope for eternal life, this is more than just a vague wish that some day we are going to dwell in the mansions of heaven. This is a confident hope. We live with the marvelous certainty that after we leave this earth we shall dwell with all fellow believers in the presence of God's glory.

Peter thus speaks of a living hope. He writes that the God and Father of our Lord Jesus Christ "has given us new birth into a living hope through the resurrection of Jesus Christ from the dead." Our living hope is very closely connected with the resurrection of Jesus. On the cross Jesus died. He was dead. But on that glorious first Easter morning he rose from the dead. He now lives. He is our living Savior who promises, "Because I live, you also will live."

Likewise we also were once dead, spiritually dead. When we came into this world we were dead in trespasses and sins. But through our new birth we are now spiritually alive. We have a living hope, a hope that is alive. We have a hope that will never fail. This gives us complete confidence that some day we shall follow our Savior in rising from the grave. How rich we are to be blessed with a living hope!

My hope is built on nothing less
Than Jesus' blood and righteousness;
I dare not trust the sweetest frame,
But wholly lean on Jesus' name.
On Christ, the solid Rock, I stand;
All other ground is sinking sand. Amen.

And I have the same hope in God as these men, that there will be a resurrection of both the righteous and the wicked. (Acts 24:15)

STAND UP WITH HOPE

To say the least, St. Paul's situation was precarious. He had been arrested and imprisoned. With the aid of a smooth-talking lawyer, the enemy had brought some very serious charges against the Apostle. Governor Felix could sentence Paul to a lengthy prison term. He could order Paul's death.

But in spite of the danger which he faced, Paul was undaunted and unafraid. Without worry or care, he boldly defended himself and his work in Felix's court.

What was the source of Paul's fearlessness and courage? In his defense before Felix Paul points to the reason for his confidence. He declares that he has "hope in God." He is sure that "there will be a resurrection of both the righteous and the wicked." So what if he must languish in prison for awhile! So what if enemies put an end to his life! Paul was confident that Jesus would raise his body from the dead and would bring him to the glory of eternal life.

In this world we too must face danger and hardship. Some people may actually threaten to kill us. Others may try to hurt our feelings, to destroy our family happiness, or to ruin us financially. Then there are the ever-present dangers of a tragic accident, a serious illness, being laid off of work, a flood, a tornado and other natural disasters.

But no matter how great the danger may be, we need not be frightened or upset, if we hold fast to Jesus in faith. Come disaster, pain or death, still we shall be "more than conquerors" through him that loved us. Jesus fills our hearts with hope. In his Word he assures us that all things, including the gravest danger and deepest sorrow, must work together for good to them that love God. Even when we "pass through the valley of the shadow of death," we need not fear any evil. Jesus will bring us safely to the other side. And we shall dwell in the house of the Lord forevermore.

In every peril and danger, let us stand up for Jesus boldly and courageously. For we have the sure hope that Jesus is at our side to defend us and to deliver us.

Lord Jesus, forgive our fears and weakness of faith. Fix our eyes on the hope of glory which you have pledged to us. Help us to stand up for you with boldness and courage. Amen.

Praise be to the God and Father of our Lord Jesus Christ! In his great mercy he has given us new birth into a living hope through the resurrection of Jesus Christ from the dead. (1 Peter 1:3)

A LIVING HOPE

"**I**'m sorry, Mrs. Lansing, there was nothing we could do." It was the evening of Christmas Day. Daniel Lansing had gone to church alone that morning while his wife and his children's families slept late. The whole family had come home for the holidays. They had eaten and talked and laughed together. And then after that evening's good-byes, Daniel sat down in his easy chair—and died.

At the funeral home, Mrs. Cheryl Lansing wrestled with the urge to cry each time someone expressed his sympathies. Yet she listened as they filed by and said, "If there's anything we can do." "He looks so natural." "We'll miss him too."

All well meaning, surely, but the pain wasn't truly lessened until— "Remember, God not only gave us Christmas, Cheryl, he also gave us Easter." Linda Danson, a neighbor from her husband's church, had come. What was that she said? "He also gave us Easter."

These words lingered long after the funeral. Rather than mailing the thank-you to Linda, Cheryl decided to walk over to her neighbor's and drop it off personally. In the middle of shoveling her front steps, Linda puffed that it was time for a break anyway. She insisted that Cheryl come in for tea or coffee. After some small talk, Cheryl asked, "What did you mean, 'He also gave us Easter'?" Linda stared at the steam rising from her cup. She was looking for divine guidance on what to say.

Linda told Cheryl of the Savior, told her how the Jesus of Christmas was the same person who later died on a cross near Jerusalem. This same Jesus actually rose from the dead on the first Easter morning. He promised an eternal life of joy in heaven to all who believe in him—as Daniel had believed.

Oh, Cheryl had heard it all before from her husband. But this time the words seemed somehow different. God was using the calling home of her husband to call her home in a different way. He reclaimed Cheryl as part of his flock through the power of his word. And now Cheryl had something she had thought during this past week she would never have again. She had hope, a living hope. Because Daniel's Savior lived—no, because THEIR Savior lived, Daniel hadn't really died. And neither would she.

My Savior, help me ever cling to the hope of the resurrection. Amen.

What we will be has not yet been made known. (1 John 3:2)

THERE IS MORE IN STORE

When we begin to add up all the blessings we enjoy as the people of God, the list just keeps on growing. We're simply overwhelmed by God's graciousness. In explaining the First Article of the Creed, Luther makes a list of blessings from God: "clothing and shoes, meat and drink, house and home, wife and children, land and cattle, and all my goods and all that I need for my body and life." And then in the Second Article Luther points to the greatest blessing: "[He] has redeemed me a lost and condemned creature."

But there is still more to come! Our text for today says that "what we shall be has not yet been made known." Doesn't that whet your appetite as to what God has in mind for us in glory?

When we consider these words of our God, a growing anticipation of glory ought to develop within us. If a father tells his child, "I have a surprise for you on Friday," can't you imagine how the youngster will grow in anticipation of what the surprise might be?

Our heavenly Father does much the same thing. He tells us that we shall live with him in glory, but he doesn't tell us much what that glory will be like. He does tell us enough to know that it is going to be most pleasant and happy.

What effect should this have on our living in this world? For one thing, it ought to be a constant reminder that in this life we occupy only temporary quarters. Our permanent home is with God in heaven. Keeping this in mind helps us maintain a proper attitude toward this world and the things of this world.

What a terrific hedge this future hope is against depression or despondency! Satan would like nothing better than to get us long-faced and feeling sorry for ourselves over the loss of some earthly possession, or over our health problems, or over personal relationships. Obviously the problems of life aren't pleasant, but neither do they snuff out our hope. This hope rests upon the promises of God, and he in no way lies or deceives. There is more in store, much more. We have God's Word on it.

Dear Lord, you have done all things right. Your creation was without flaw. Your redemption of all men is perfect and complete. And beyond this you hold before us a promise of even more blessings to come. Keep us living in faith and trust through all the trials of this life. Help us to realize that the sufferings of today cannot diminish the beauty and joy of what you have in store for us. We ask this through your Son, Jesus Christ, our Lord. Amen.

Dear friends, now we are children of God, and what we will be has not yet been made known. But we know that when he appears, we shall be like him, for we shall see him as he is. (1 John 3:2)

ANTICIPATING HEAVENLY JOY

What will heaven be like? From what Scripture tells us, heaven is a place of perfect joy and happiness. It is interesting to note, however, that Scripture often speaks of heaven in terms of what will not be there. This is because we are sinful human beings living in a sinful world. We have not experienced perfect joy and happiness, and we cannot imagine what that will be like. Scripture speaks in terms of sin with all its sorrows being absent from heaven. This gives us a picture of what our heavenly existence will be.

St. John received a revelation of the new heaven and the new earth. He described it as a place where all sin is removed. Death, mourning, crying and pain will be things of the past. Believers will live eternally in the presence of their loving Savior. John said of those in heaven, "They are before the throne of God and serve him day and night in his temple; and he who sits on the throne will spread his tent over them. Never again will they hunger; never again will they thirst. The sun will not beat upon them, nor any scorching heat. For the Lamb at the center of the throne will be their shepherd; he will lead them to springs of living water. And God will wipe away every tear from their eyes" (Revelation 7:15-17).

In heaven we will be confirmed in holiness, freed from the corruption of sin so we may serve our Lord forever in righteousness. We shall have the same bodies, but they will be glorified, patterned after the glorious resurrection body of Jesus.

What glory we have to look forward to! What joy will be ours! Yet, this joy also serves us now. In this life our eyes are often clouded with tears. Because we live in a world corrupted by sin, we experience pain and heartache. When we become burdened by the problems of this life, we need to remember the words of John, "Dear friends, now we are children of God . . . But when he appears, we shall be like him." We have joy that makes life worth living. We have hope that takes the fear out of dying. Praise the God of our salvation for the hope he has given us!

O sweet and blessed country, the home of God's elect!
O sweet and blessed country that eager hearts expect!
Jesus, in mercy bring us to that dear land of rest,
Who art, with God the Father and Spirit, ever blest. Amen.

And we know that in all things God works for the good of those who love him, who have been called according to his purpose. For those God foreknew he also predestined to be conformed to the likeness of his Son, that he might be the firstborn among many brothers. And those he predestined, he also called; those he called, he also justified; those he justified, he also glorified. (Romans 8:28-30)

I'M SURE!

"George, if you should die today, will you go to heaven?" "Yes," replied George. "You can't be absolutely sure, can you?" asked his friend. "I'm sure! and I'll tell you why I'm so very sure."

God invited me to be his child. He did this through the good news of the Gospel which tells me of my salvation in Jesus. He has seen to it that I have not only heard but have also accepted his invitation. He has caused my heart and mind to accept the invitation. In this way faith that trusts in Jesus for salvation was created in me. Because of this faith, God is no longer angry with me over sin. My God-given faith takes the righteousness of Christ and makes me holy and just in God's eyes. That's how I was made his child.

As his child I'm sure that everything that happens to me will serve for my good and lead me yet closer to the Lord. You see, God will let no harm come to any of his children. In fact, it has to be this way. Before time began, God knew me and decided that I was to become his child. Therefore he provided a way for my salvation in Jesus. He saw to it that I was invited and called to be his child through his holy Word. He moved my heart to accept and believe the invitation. He is actually keeping me in faith right now through his Word. That's why I have faith that trusts in Jesus' blood and righteousness. That's why I am his child. That's why I have a sacred promise from him.

Our gracious Lord, who made me his child through faith in Jesus, has made me a sacred promise. He has promised that he will glorify me, that is, make and keep me perfect for heaven. So it's just a matter of time until he will also give me the perfect reason for his inviting and calling me. In heaven his promise will be kept.

"Yes, dear friend, I'm sure I will go to heaven when I die. God has taken the whole matter out of my hands and has given me the gift of eternal life. Oh, how he loves me! You're his child by faith in Jesus. You too can be sure," encouraged George, as he was taken to the operating room where God kept his sacred promise to him.

O Lord, truly you have loved us. Amen.

Not only so, but we also rejoice in our sufferings, because we know that suffering produces perseverance; perseverance, character; and character, hope. And hope does not disappoint us, because God has poured out his love into our hearts by the Holy Spirit, whom he has given us. (Romans 5:3-5)

OUR JOY AMID TRIBULATION

In this sin-cursed world in which we live, things don't always turn out the way we plan. As a result our hearts are often filled with sorrow, disappointment and fear. But what a comfort it is to know that we have a Savior who can say, "I know exactly how you feel. I faced those same hardships during my life on earth." It's with a full personal understanding of all our problems that our Savior graciously invites us, "Come to me, all you who are weary and burdened, and I will give you rest."

But we've never seen Jesus. We've never actually heard him speak to us. How can we receive strength and comfort from someone whom we've never seen or heard? That's the work and function of the Holy Ghost. The Holy Ghost comforts us in all our tribulations by directing our attention to the loving concern which Jesus has expressed for us in his Word.

Are you a young person who sometimes wonders, "Could Jesus possibly know and understand how I feel?" Remember the rich young ruler? The Bible shows that Jesus understood that young man better than that young man understood himself. Are you growing old and feeling concerned that you're becoming a burden to your loved ones? Jesus can understand this concern. Didn't he appoint John to care for his mother so that she wouldn't feel unloved and unwanted in her twilight years! Have you lost a loved one in death? Jesus knows the feeling. He wept at the grave of Lazarus. Jesus knows the feeling of being so completely exhausted from work that one can barely keep one's eyes open. He knows the feeling of pain. Yes, he even knows what it feels like to die, for remember, he died for our sin.

It was the Holy Spirit who inspired the apostles to record all these feelings of Jesus in the Scriptures, in order to assure us that Jesus knows what we feel and is able to meet our needs. By bringing us the good news about Jesus' great love for us, the Holy Spirit fills our hearts with the strength needed to face all our problems with patience, hope and joy.

Above all, Jesus took our sins away. He removed that which would make our tribulations unbearable. That's how much he loved us!

Holy Spirit, in all my tribulations comfort me with the good news of Jesus' love for me. Amen.

If we have been united with him like this in his death, we will certainly also be united with him in his resurrection. (Romans 6:5)

CERTAIN TO RISE

What is certain in this life of ours? "Death and taxes," the cynic replies. "Everything else changes." Families grow up. Cities sprout suburbs. Bulldozers level houses for parking lots. Idled factories become upscale condominiums. A lot of people don't even know where their next meal is coming from. What is certain?

For the Christian it is not only death that is certain. We can be certain to rise on the last day to everlasting life. That is because we have been united with Christ. By faith God has completely joined the life of his Son and our lives together.

When a gardener grafts a branch to the tree, he expects that graft to take hold and receive its nourishment through the tree. If the tree suffers damage in either its trunk or root system, the graft will also suffer. The graft shares the life of the tree.

Or consider a hot-air balloon. The basket in which the balloonist rides does not soar through the sky without the balloon. If the balloon plunges to the ground, certainly the basket will also follow. One destiny awaits both.

Jesus Christ is the tree to which we have been grafted by God's grace through faith. Whatever Jesus experiences, we will experience. The same destiny is ours.

Jesus really died on the cross to take our sins away. It is historical fact. We are sure it happened. Easter is another historical fact. We believe that Jesus rose from the dead. Because he rose, we will rise. Jesus promised. His promises are sure.

Our certainty can be just that, and not wishful thinking. We base our hopes not upon the changing nature of this world or upon the fickle people who fill this world. We base our hopes upon our eternal and unchanging Lord Jesus Christ. We have been united with him in his death by faith. We will certainly also be united with him in life everlasting.

Heavenly Father, give me the certainty that, just as my Savior Jesus rose from the dead, I too will rise on the last day and spend eternity with you in heaven. Amen.

For I am convinced that (nothing) . . . will be able to separate us from the love of God that is in Christ Jesus our Lord. (Romans 8:38,39)

A FRIEND ON OUR SIDE

Let's pretend that I am a small child. I am not gifted with a great amount of natural ability or physical strength. Now, let's pretend that right down the street from me there live three other children. They are the neighborhood bullies. They are big, and they are strong. They have also told me that they are not particularly fond of me. In fact, they have told me that the next time they see me downtown, they are going to pick a fight.

Now let's pretend that one day my mother asks me to go to the store for her. How would I feel? Probably not very good, right? I would want to do what my mother asks, and yet I am afraid because of the threats I have received. I am not sure if I can overcome that problem by myself.

But then, just when things seem to be at their worst, my uncle comes to visit. He is big, and he is strong. Nothing frightens him. He looks at me and says, "Come on, I'll go along with you to the store." How would I feel then? Not so frightened anymore, right?

Why not? Because I have a big, strong, powerful friend right beside me. I know that as long as he is there, none of the bullies will bother me. So I walk down the street with a definite feeling of security, with a newfound sense of confidence. I have nothing to fear. I am convinced of that.

Have you ever felt that way in the course of your lifetime? Sometimes the problems, the pains and the persecutions of this life seem to squeeze us so tightly. We seem so terribly weak and powerless. We are frightened. We don't think that we can overcome those bullies by ourselves. And we are probably correct. By ourselves we cannot.

But fortunately for us as Christians we don't have to overcome them by ourselves. We have a big, strong, powerful ally and friend. He does the fighting for us. And he is not just someone who visits us every now and then. He is with us every day of our lives. This is his promise. We can now be secure with nothing to fear. We, like Paul, are convinced of that fact.

Heavenly Father, be with us and give us courage to face and to overcome any problems that plague us. Amen.

Though you have not seen him, you love him; and even though you do not see him now, you believe In him. (1 Peter 1:8)

THANK GOD YOU BELIEVE

"**W**e would like to see Jesus," some Greeks said to Philip the disciple. They wanted to see and meet personally this man of whom they had heard such wonderful things.

Every Christian has the same longing—to see Jesus. Perhaps it is in our most difficult moments that we most wish we could see Jesus. The sight of our glorified Savior would do so much for us, we think.

Maybe sometimes we envy those women, those disciples, even Thomas, the doubter, who were privileged to see the risen Lord with their own eyes. How much stronger we'd be if we could have the same opportunity!

But that's really not necessary, is it? The marvelous thing about faith is that it clings to the unseen. The disciples saw Jesus because they were to be the eyewitnesses who would pass on what they had seen to others, including us. Not all need to see him. But everyone needs to hear about him.

Remember what our Savior said to Thomas, "Blessed are those who have not seen and yet have believed." Certainly Peter had that in mind as he wrote the words of today's text. He knew that sight is not necessary for faith. Faith in God and in Christ can exist perfectly well without seeing. "Faith is being sure of what we hope for and certain of what we do not see," the writer to the Hebrews reminds us. We should also remember that there were many, like the scribes and Pharisees, who did see Jesus on earth but still refused to believe in him.

Though we have not seen our Savior with our own eyes, we love him, for we have heard about his love and sacrifice for us. Even though we don't see him, we still believe in him, for by God's Word and Spirit we have received the gift of faith.

We would indeed like to see Jesus. And one day we will. But until then we can thank and praise our God that we believe without seeing, that we know our Savior as well and love him as the disciples who followed him during his ministry. Until we do see him, we are confident that:

Blessed are they that have not seen
And yet whose faith hath constant been;
In life eternal they shall reign.

Lord Jesus, our crucified and risen Redeemer, accept our thanks and praise for faith, life and salvation. Keep us in that faith until we see you with our own eyes in glory. Amen.

We . . . rejoice in God through our Lord Jesus Christ, through whom we have now received reconciliation. (Romans 5:11)

LOVE BRINGS TRUE JOY

Happiness, it is said, is a state of mind. Some days that state of mind is nowhere to be found. Observe the faces of those who pass you on the sidewalk. Some look as if they had eaten ground glass for breakfast. Even at a funeral you won't see faces that long.

Perhaps it's understandable. Our economic picture doesn't always promote happiness. Homeowners live under the burden of having to pay one bill after another. A river of depressing news threatens to drown us each day: the soaring crime rate, child abuse, political scandal, illegal drugs, marital unfaithfulness, energy and environmental crises—all add heavy weights to the strains under which we live. No wonder ours deserves to be dubbed the aspirin age.

In times like these even Christians are prone to depression, lured to seek relief in shallow, worldly cures. The final words of our lesson, however, are an invitation to find true joy in our God and his Word. Still, this joy is hard to feel. Why?

When we sense that someone is holding something against us, we go on the defensive and are even tempted to become hostile. This is even more true of our relationship with God. If things are not going well, if illness or financial setbacks or other personal problems are threatening us, we are tempted to think that God is punishing us for our sins. But that is not the case with God's children. As Paul tells us, "God was reconciling the world to himself in Christ, not counting men's sins against them." God does not hold our sins against us anymore. So complete is our reconciliation in Christ that God feels nothing but the warmest love for us. He gives us his peace, the strength to rejoice even in trials, the secure hope of salvation.

Only the knowledge of this love of God can quiet the Christian's heart when it is troubled. When a lake is deep, storms may ruffle the surface waters, but below all is calm. Life will test our spirits too, but if we immerse our thoughts in the depths of God's love, we will still rejoice, even when we must weep. "Though you have not seen him, you love him; and even though you do not see him now, you believe in him and are filled with an inexpressible and glorious joy, for you are receiving the goal of your faith, the salvation of your souls" (1 Peter 1:8,9).

Dear Lord, we rejoice in you. Give us power to express that joy in the way that we live. Hear us, for Jesus' sake. Amen..

And do not grieve the Holy Spirit of God, with whom you were sealed for the day of redemption. (Ephesians 4:30)

SEALED WITH THE HOLY SPIRIT

These inspired words of the sacred writer are some of the most comforting words in Scripture. We are "sealed" with the Holy Spirit "for the day of redemption." Sealed is a legal term. The seal makes valid the statement of a person. The seal guarantees it. Probably for the majority of us Christians, this sealing occurred already in our baptism when as babies we were brought into God's family. For others it may have occurred later, when they came to faith as adults. In either event, the Lord assures us that this seal will stand to the last great day, when we will be freed from sin and death and be his forever in heaven.

Because we have this seal, this assurance of God that we are his no matter what, he will be with us and keep us to the very last day. What a tremendously powerful defense this knowledge is against temptations and against the attacks of Satan, who wants us to think that our faith is uncertain and our future shaky.

Regardless of what happens, we can be sure we are God's. He has sealed us as his own in the Spirit. That is the most wonderful knowledge, and we need to hang on to it.

When we get up in the morning, when we are about the business of the day, when we are lying down at night, we know that we are in God's hands because he has sealed us to be his own. He is by our side with his gracious will and his almighty power. The Bible assures us that "the Lord knows those who are his." He knows us and keeps us in his love.

What a surge of joy, power, gratitude and praise is ours, as we understand that we are sealed for the day of redemption! The burden of feeling that the future of our faith depends on our own strength is lifted. We know our own strength is not dependable. But the Spirit of God works through the means of grace with his almighty power. In that we can feel safe and secure!

God does not want us to use this feeling of security in our faith to become indifferent toward sin. Rather, he wants to provide comfort amid times of helplessness and feelings of despair. And he gives us motivation when he assures us that we are sealed by the Spirit. Knowing that we belong to God, we will want to live as his children.

Dear Holy Spirit, I am so happy in the knowledge that you have sealed me. You have assured me that it is your almighty power that will keep me in the faith to the last day. For this I praise you. Amen.

He cares for you. (1 Peter 5:7)

GOD CARES

Every once in a while something may happen to make us wonder whether anyone really is concerned about us or not. Do we mean anything to anyone? Or are we just numbers on a charge card, a license plate, a social security card?

It is not unusual suddenly to discover that there are more people who have a real concern for us than we ever imagined. But it is also true that there is no one who has a greater interest in us and a greater concern for us than God does.

It should hardly be necessary for Peter to write as he does and to say: "He cares for you." For isn't this apparent from personal experience? When day after day God supplies, not only what we need, but far more; when we find joy in our work and God crowns our labors with a measure of success; when in the morning we arise from a refreshing sleep and when in the evening we return home safely; doesn't all of this say simply but eloquently: "He cares for you." And then we look back over our past and see how God has watched over us

and led us to this very hour. Perhaps now we can see to an extent how he is able to bring good out of those times of suffering and sorrow. Once again we are reminded that God cares about us.

More important than all of these things, God has also given us his Word. There we learn how God in love chose us from all eternity to be his own, and how, to make this a blessed reality, he sent his own Son to be our Savior, to give his life for us. At the cross of Calvary, more than anywhere else, we see God's matchless love—a love that forgives, a love that restores to us eternal life.

Because of what Jesus has done for us, God is no longer angry with us. He is pleased to send his holy angels to watch over us. He guides the flow of history so that men will not be able to rob us of our salvation. He restrains the power of Satan, closes the gates of hell and opens the gates of heaven for us.

No, it should not have been necessary for Peter to write as he did. But that we might not doubt it even in our darkest hour, God had him say it once more: "He cares for you."

My spirit on Thy care,
Blest Savior, I recline;
Thou wilt not leave me to despair,
For Thou art Love divine. Amen.

Who shall separate us from the love of Christ? (Romans 8:35)

CHRIST'S LOVE IS OUR SECURITY

We need security, but so often we feel very insecure. We hang our need for security on some very thin wires at times. Take our health, for example. People who have that wide, vertical, zipper-like scar down the middle of their chests are living proof that we are all only a pulse beat this side away from that side. Something as tiny as a blood clot, smaller, much smaller than a pea, if lodged in the wrong place, can suddenly turn our speech into a slur and reduce our steps to a shuffle or less.

We hang the heavy need for security on the thin wire of our possessions. We know better, but we still do it. Materialistic to the core, we convince ourselves that life does consist in the abundance of the things we possess, that contentment is not limited to food and clothing, that birds of the air and lilies of the field don't know what they're missing without all these creature comforts. Enter layoffs and medical bills and unexpected expenses. Exit the comfortable savings account and the financial plan. Snap goes the wire on our security.

Or the thin wire may be familiarity and predictability. We feel secure with the same job, the same house, the same school, the same family, and on and on. Enter the corporation take-over, graduation, a new political regime. Snap goes the wire. All the above have their good places in our life, but they don't give us what we ultimately need.

"Who shall separate us from the love of Christ?" asks the Apostle Paul. His answer is clearly implied. No one and and no thing. God's love shown to us in Christ is the sturdy cable on which we can hang our need for security.

Christ's love is universal. "God so loved the world." There is no need for us to fear that we are excepted from this love.

Christ's love is unchanging. "Jesus Christ is the same yesterday and today and forever." There is no need to fear that his love will disappear at some future time.

Christ's love is unconditional. "While we were still sinners, Christ died for us." We can reject Christ's love, but never destroy it. It is there for us always. It offers us forgiveness and life, as well as the security we long for and need to have.

O Lord Jesus, we thank you for your love which is given to us and never taken from us. Help us rely upon it always. Amen.

My message and my preaching were not with wise and persuasive words, but with a demonstration of the Spirit's power, so that your faith might not rest on men's wisdom, but on God's power. (1 Corinthians 2:4,5)

RELYING ON GOD'S POWER

At times Paul presented a rather negative picture of himself as he preached at Corinth. Recall what he said of himself: "I did not come with eloquence or superior wisdom. . . . I came to you in weakness and fear, and with much trembling. My message and my preaching were not with wise and persuasive words." From just this description of his preaching we might expect to learn that all his hearers were disappointed, bored and totally turned off.

But they were not. The book of Acts tells us, "Many of the Corinthians who heard him believed and were baptized." Why? Was it because they were so impressed with the man Paul? Obviously not. It doesn't seem there was much in his appearance, style or vocabulary to be impressed about. Only because of the power of God did the Corinthians know of their salvation in Christ after hearing Paul preach.

From A to Z our salvation is the powerful work of God. He planned it. He worked it out at the cross by his Son. His inspired Word tells us of it and invites us to receive it. By the power of his Spirit we are led to accept the great news of our forgiveness and are kept in the saving faith. That's why we can be positive of our salvation. It is based 100 percent on God's power. What confidence that marvelous fact gives!

Faith that relies on people can sometimes disappoint us. We may have had the rug pulled out from under us when we thought we could trust someone. A friend who sends us a valentine one day might disappoint us the next.

It could even happen that the pastor from whom we learned the Word of God might later reject God's Word. Certainly that would shock us and disappoint us. But it would not place our salvation in jeopardy. Our faith does not rest on men, "but on God's power."

Rely on your faithful God's power, and you have every reason to be certain of your salvation. He cannot disappoint.

Thank you, Lord, for the assurance that from beginning to end my salvation is your powerful work. Now I may serve you in confidence and tonight rest secure through Jesus Christ our Lord. Amen.